Bottom Line Financial Planning

Manage Risk And Fund The Good Life... Your Whole Life

Kenny Gott, CFP®, SPHR
with John Piatchek, CLU, ChFC

Huge Tune Publishing

Copyright © 2017 Kenny Gott.

Cover art © 2017 Andie Bottrell

All rights reserved.
ISBN-13: 978-1505877304
ISBN-10: 150587730X

Contact us at Piatchek & Associates, Springfield, MO. 417-881-7900, and visit PiatchekAndAssociates.com to learn more about us and our financial planning services.

Securities offered through Kestra Investment Services, LLC (Kestra IS), member FINRA/SIPC. Investment Advisory Services offered through Kestra Advisory Services, LLC (Kestra AS), and affiliate of Kestra IS. Piatchek & Associates is a member of PartnersFinancial. Kestra IS and Kestra AS are not affiliated with Piatchek & Associates, PartnersFinancial or any other entity listed. Kestra IS and Kestra AS do not provide tax or legal advice.

To ensure compliance with requirements imposed by the IRS under Circular 230, we inform you that any U.S. Federal tax advice contained in this communication, unless otherwise specifically stated, was not intended or written to be used, and cannot be used, for the purpose of (1) avoiding penalties under the Internal Revenue Code or (2) promoting, marketing, or recommending to another party any matters addressed herein.

Mutual funds and variable annuities are sold by prospectus only. Before investing, investors should carefully consider the investment objectives, risks, charges and expenses of a mutual fund, or a variable annuity and its underlying investment options. For mutual funds, the fund prospectus, and for variable annuities, the current contract prospectus and underlying fund prospectuses, provide this and other important information. Please contact your representative or the Company to obtain a prospectus. Please read the prospectus(es) carefully before investing or sending money. All investments involve varying levels and types of risks. These risks can be associated with the specific investment, or with the marketplace as a whole. Loss of principal is possible. The opinions expressed in this book are those of the author and may not necessarily reflect those held by Kestra Investment Services, LLC or Kestra Advisory Services, LLC. This is for general information only and is not intended to provide specific investment advice or recommendations for any individual. It is suggested that you consult your financial professional, attorney, or tax advisor with regard to your individual situation. Any comments concerning past performance are not intended to be forward looking and should not be viewed as an indication of future results. Any hypothetical case study results or illustrations are for illustrative purposes only and should not be deemed a representation of past or future results. The examples do not represent any specific product, nor do they reflect sales charges or other expenses that may be required for some investments. No representation is made as to the accurateness of the analysis.

Acknowledgements

Sincere thanks to our clients for entrusting us with their financial concerns, and for teaching us as much about life as we teach them about financial planning.

Thanks to Kenny's mom Paula Gott and our Client Relations Manager Andie Bottrell for editing assistance—including keeping one eye on whether we met our goal of explaining every concept as clearly and simply as possible. Special thanks to Andie for her lovely cover painting.

Thanks to Joe Piatchek for his estate planning expertise, and to Audrey Bottrell for her valuable input in the Medicare section.

Thanks to colleagues Dennis "Bud" Page and Stephen Evans for always being great sources of information and wisdom (and good friends).

Thanks to Deanna Wheeler, Tina Gott, and Andie for creating an exceptional experience for our clients. Our practice, and this book, would not be the same without you.

Finally, thanks to our family for their perpetual love and support.

*For Tina and Amanda,
and our extended family (our clients).*

Introduction

Our practice (Piatchek & Associates in Springfield, Missouri) has helped hundreds of families, individuals, and business owners with their financial concerns since 1972. Our wonderful clients are of all ages and backgrounds, and we're in the business of helping each of them manage risk and achieve their dreams. We take that mission very seriously—we want our clients to have a better experience with us than they could get anywhere else.

We believe an important reason we're successful in this mission is that we start with the fundamentals with each client—making sure they understand basic financial planning concepts that relate to their goals. Many new clients have told us that we explain these "bottom line" essentials in a simpler, clearer way than our competitors.

The "bottom line" gets to the point, cuts to the chase—skips the B.S. if you'll pardon the expression. Its original meaning relates to tax accounting: "top line" items are before exclusions and deductions; the "bottom line" is the total on which taxes are owed. So this title may be particularly appropriate for a book about keeping—and potentially growing—more of what's yours, and figuring out what to do with it.

We do discuss tax concepts, as our mantra for income planning is "make it last, pay less taxes"...but we believe there's a whole lot more to planning for a comfortable life, and a comfortable retirement.

Our Financial Blueprint process helps our clients, and us, clarify life goals and financial goals, and the actions needed to help attain those goals. We encourage you to adopt this "fiscal house" analogy because it works, and because it helps bring perspective to the importance of having a solid financial structure to help you meet your goals. For most of us, our house is our most valuable asset, and if we're fortunate, provides both shelter and comfort. Your financial plan may also provide both. Lack of planning could destroy both.

The foundation of your home needs to be strong and properly designed to support the entire structure above it, and in this book we lay out basics that should be considered for your financial plan, regardless of whether you have a little to work with or a lot.

But building a house yourself would be a huge undertaking. Not many people have the knowledge or skills (or the licenses) to be their own architect, general contractor, plumber, electrician, roofer, or to wear the many other hats required to design and construct a house.

Fortunately there are professionals who can help. Some people enjoy rolling up their sleeves to drive a few nails themselves, but the only happy task you're absolutely required to handle is figuring out what you want your dream house to look like—the size and location of the rooms, the arrangement of the kitchen, safety features, conveniences, cosmetics—and convey your wishes to your team of specialists who can make your vision a reality.

Your financial house may be just as complicated as your physical home...and the hazards of a do-it-yourself approach may be just as disastrous. Our old friend Rick said it best many years ago, in his long Arkansas drawl: "The truth is, it ain't just what you don't know that'll hurt you—it's what you don't know, that you *think* you know."

The good news is that basic financial planning concepts are understandable to the average person, at least in the broad strokes, and with the assistance of a solid team your vision of your financial life can really happen. On budget. On time.

But first your vision needs to be *informed* and *organized*.

The following chapters will help guide you through the basic elements of a sound fiscal structure. We've tried to organize the material in a way that enables you to find items of most concern to you as you prioritize your goals and worries.

Each chapter starts with these "bottom line" guideposts:

"The Bottom Line": a nutshell summary of planning items to consider. Not every item applies to every client's situation (for example we include information for business owners)—but each one which *does* apply to your circumstances is critically important. We include additional "bottom line" summaries at the beginning of some sections within chapters.

"The Team": A listing of specialty advisors you may need to consult for a potentially better outcome.

"Do-Some-Of-It-Yourselfers": Items you may reasonably be able to handle with a little research and elbow grease…along with pitfalls to watch for, and an occasional firm warning against even attempting to do some things yourself.

"How it works in the real world": Stories from our practice…real people, real issues, real solutions based on concepts that follow.

From there you may want to skim the Table Of Contents to find specific planning points most relevant to your situation, or just read the whole book—we've tried to keep it concise and interesting, not too far in the weeds, and broadly relevant.

We have developed our understanding of these basic financial planning concepts over many years of helping clients resolve their financial concerns. We hope you enjoy and benefit from this information, and we wish you well as you watch your brand new fiscal house take shape.

John and Kenny

Contents

1. **Building A Plan**.. 1
   - About The Team.. 5
   - What To Look For In A Financial Advisor................................... 6
     - Fiduciary... 6
     - Designations... 8
     - Ethics... 10
     - Communication Style And Compatibility........................ 12
     - Scope.. 13
     - Transparency (Advisor Compensation)........................... 16
   - Advisor Hazards... 23
   - A Word About Independent vs. "Captive" Advisors................... 24

   - The Planning Process... 25
     - Goal Setting... 25
     - The Initial Inspection: What's In The Junk Drawer?........ 27
     - Developing Recommendations.. 28
     - Implementing The Plan... 30
     - Monitoring Progress, And Reviews................................. 30

   - Special Planning Considerations For Couples......................... 32
   - Getting Your Financial Act Together (Not Just For Couples)...33
   - Special Planning Considerations For Business Owners........ 35

2. **Income, Budget, and Accumulation Planning**........................ 37
   - Your Budget: Analyzing Expenses... 41
   - The "Earn More" Side Of The Budget Equation........................ 41
   - Budget Planning: Basic Living Expenses................................. 42
   - Budget Planning: "Lifestyle" Expenses..................................... 44
   - Debt Management... 45
     - "Cheap Debt" Arbitrage... 45
     - Debt Free By Choice: Sweating The Small Stuff............ 47
     - Debt Free By Choice: Sweat The Big Stuff Too!............. 48
     - Debt Management Ratios.. 49
     - To Refinance Or Not To Refinance?................................ 49
     - Stretch It Out Or Knock It Out?....................................... 50

   - Accumulation Planning... 52
     - The Wish List.. 52
     - Pay Yourself First... 53
     - Earmark Windfalls.. 53
     - Emergency Savings Accumulation.................................. 54
     - College Savings Accumulation.. 55
     - Cars And Guitars...And The "Place-Keeper".................. 59
   - Building Your Legacy.. 60

3. **Risk Management**... 61
    The Four Ways To Manage Risk... 64

    Risk Management Critical Zone I: Emergency Fund........................ 65
        Sources Of Emergency Money.. 67
        An Emergency Fund For Your Emergency Fund?................. 68

    Risk Management Critical Zone II: Health Care................................ 68
        When Is A High Health Insurance Deductible Better?.......... 70
        Health Savings Account: Quadruple Tax Play.................... 71
        Health Savings Account: IRA Supercharger For Age 65+.... 73
        Health Care Outside The Box.. 73
        Take Some Healthy Tax Breaks....................................... 74
        Medicare.. 74

    Risk Management Critical Zone III: Life Insurance............................ 78
        Buy Now!... 79
        Uses Of Life Insurance Death Benefit Proceeds................. 79
        Term Life Insurance: "Renting" Protection......................... 82
        Permanent Life Insurance: "Owning" Protection, And A
            Roth-Like Feature... 82
        The Permanent Life Insurance Four-Quadrant Win............ 85
        Life Insurance As An Enforced Savings Plan..................... 87
        Taxation Of Life Insurance.. 87
        The Life Insurance Triangle Of Doom.............................. 88
        Questions You Must Ask Your Life Insurance Agent........... 89
        A Life Insurance Strategy For "Lazy" Or "Crazy" Money...... 91

    Risk Management Critical Zone IV: Disability Insurance..................... 93

        Risk Management Critical Zone V: Property/Casualty Insurance 96
        Umbrella Liability Coverage... 98

    Risk Management Critical Zone VI: Long-Term Care Insurance........... 98
        What Types Of Long-Term Care Facilities Are Covered?..... 104
        A Long-term Care Insurance Alternative........................ 105

    Risk Management Critical Zone VII: Identity Theft And Scam Protection 107

    Risk Management For Business Owners......................................110

4. **Investing**.. 113
    Tired Of The Stock Market Roller Coaster?................................... 118
    Investment Risk And Your Risk Tolerance.................................... 119
    Systematic Investment Risk: Can't Stop This!................................ 120
    Unsystematic Risk: Diversify, Diversify, Diversify!........................... 121

Risk Tolerance: Gut Check, Or Math Problem?.. 122
What's Your Recession Reserve™?.. 123
"Sequence Of Returns" Danger.. 128
Be A Disciplined Investor... 132
Invest Efficiently... 136
Way Too Much Of A Good Thing.. 139
Investment Tax Efficiency: 401(k)'s, 403(b)'s, IRA'S...And
    "Non-Qualified" Investments... 140

Capital Gains Are Great! Capital Gains Tax, Not So Much.................. 144
When Is Selling Low A Good Thing?.. 145
Annuities... 146
The Four Types Of Annuities.. 148
Income-Producing Investments (And Their Tax Ramifications)............ 152
Rental Real Estate: You're The Landlord!... 159
Speculative Investments—And Is Gold Safe Or Speculative?................ 162
Do-It-Yourself-Investor Dangers... 163
Special Investing Considerations For Business Owners....................... 165

5. Tax Management... **167**
Let's Not Repeat Ourselves Too Much (a book-wide index of tax tips)... 170
The Ultimate Tax Break: Tax Credits... 172
The Next Best Thing To A Tax Credit: Tax Deduction.......................... 174
Charitable Tax Deductions.. 175
Accelerated Deductions... 176
The Power Of Tax Deferral And Tax-Free Spending............................. 176
Social Security Taxation.. 177
Self-Employment Tax... 178
A Word To All Business Owners... 180
Alternative Minimum Tax (AMT) Tips.. 180
Trust Tax... 182
Kiddie Tax... 183
Passive Activity And At-Risk Rules For Investors And Landlords......... 183
How Long Should You Keep Tax Records?.. 185
Tax treatment of investments: see Investing chapter
IRA beneficiary tax considerations: see Estate Planning chapter

6. Estate Planning.. **186**
The Estate Tax Exclusion Pendulum.. 190
Intra-Family Gifting.. 192
Life Insurance As A Source Of Estate Liquidity..................................... 193
Nothing Should Go Through Probate!... 194
Special Titling For Special Married Couples... 196
Powers Of Attorney... 197

Wills And Trusts (Dump Truck Or Courier Service?)............................199
The Power Of Stepped-Up Basis... 203
IRA Beneficiaries (Including Tax Considerations).............................. 204
Estate Planning For Business Owners... 208
An Estate Planning Cautionary Tale.. 209

7. **Retirement Planning**... 211
   "I Wish We Hadn't Saved So Much For Retirement..."........................215
   If You Are Not Yet Close To Retirement..216
   Retirement Accumulation Planning.. 217
   If You're Getting Close To Retirement, Or Already Retired... 220
   "Big 10" Retirement Planning Components....................................... 220
   Don't Jump The Gun On Drawing From Tax-Deferred Accounts!...........229
   The Mother Of All Tax Penalties: Missing Your RMD's........................ 229
   Social Security Maximization: The $779,000 Question........................231
   Spousal Social Security Claiming Strategies..................................... 232
   Social Security "Break-Even" Analysis... 232
   The Fatal Journey To The Mailbox... 233
   Working v. Social Security Offset..233
   Leverage A Strong Dollar For Cheap Vacations In Retirement!.............. 234
   Retirement And Succession Planning For Business Owners.................234
   We Have Bad News...And Good News..235

A Final Word.. 239

APPENDIX: The Budget List... 241

About The Author... 249

1.

Building A Plan

You wouldn't build a home without a blueprint...you shouldn't plan your financial future without one either.

-John Piatchek

BOTTOM LINE: *Have a financial plan at every stage of your life, aligned to your goals and your resources.*

As soon as you question your ability to handle any aspect of your plan competently yourself, get professional assistance. Work with a team of advisors with whom you're compatible. Research their qualifications, experience, track record, and professional designations.

Seek an independent financial advisor instead of a "captive" advisor. Understand how your advisor is paid, and be clear on the scope of your planning engagement with each of your advisors.

Familiarize yourself with the general steps of the financial planning process. Understand the products and processes you and your advisor will use to fulfill your plan. Ask questions.

For couples: be aware of planning issues specific to your situation.

For business owners: you have special considerations for every financial planning area—seek experienced professional guidance.

For everyone: organize your finances and records in a way that will help your survivors pick up the pieces more easily and effectively if you die unexpectedly.

THE TEAM

Almost everyone needs sooner or later:
Financial planning professional
Investment professional (some but not all CFP®, ChFC or other financial planning professionals are qualified for this role).
Accountant
Attorney
Life insurance professional
Property and casualty insurance professional
Health insurance professional

And in some life stages:
Medicare supplement agent
Long-term care insurance professional

And for some:
Real estate broker/agent
Business planning specialists (see each chapter for details)

DO-SOME-OF-IT-YOURSELFERS: You are responsible for as much of the heavy lifting as anyone on your team, because it really is *your* future, and *your* goals, and nobody on the team except you can figure out what that needs to look like. You have to dig deep sometimes to get clear on what the "good life" really means to you.

Some have gone as far as to fulfill part or even all of the education requirements for professional certification just for the sake of their own planning. Without also having the experience requirement for certification—years of on-the-ground financial planning, working through hundreds of real-life scenarios and learning subtle and complex pathways through the financial underbrush—you should still seek professional advice.

But the more knowledge you have, the better your results may be. So be open to new information, ask questions, and don't worry if you don't have the time or energy to study for the exams—your advisor already did that for you!

How it works in the real world: We enjoy presenting educational workshops for the public, and meeting privately at our office with attendees who request a consultation. One couple we'll call Mr. and Mrs. R brought in their investment statements from a well-known "big box" company and asked if they could do better.

We agreed to provide an investment analysis, but we had a few other questions first. As usual we asked about other critical financial planning areas in order to better understand how their investments fit into their overall picture, as nothing in the financial life of a couple exists in a vacuum.

When we asked about their risk management preparations, in particular their long-term care planning, Mrs. R said, "Let me tell you—I asked our current investment advisor the same thing. She held up our quarterly investment statement and said, "Well…this *is* your long-term care plan!""

Mr. and Mrs. R recognized that this wasn't a very good answer. We hear stories like this all too often; many advisors are not interested in delving into comprehensive financial planning areas, or are simply not qualified to do so. And a surprising number of them don't even recognize when a client simply needs a referral to a specialist.

We explained that Missouri is one of several states which offer some protection of assets from Medicaid spend-down rules for people who purchase a qualifying long-term care insurance policy. We offered to arrange a meeting with one of our associates, a long-term care specialist who could educate them about their options.

Other issues came up in this meeting—their current advisor had needlessly cost them a significant amount of capital gains tax during the current year; worst of all they had no long-term income strategy and Mrs. R was very worried about being a good steward of the inheritance her father left her.

We explained that we can certainly help manage their investments, in addition to addressing their other concerns—starting with the issues that were of most concern to them.

Mrs. R looked at her husband and said, "It looks like we don't just need an investment advisor. We need a financial planner."

On their way out the door Mr. R hung back briefly, leaned in close and whispered, "The only thing I care about is that she's taken care of after I'm gone."

These moments mean more to us than we can tell you. We know we're dealing with real people with real concerns…and that our guidance may lead them to imagine a better life, and build a better life. What an awesome and wonderful responsibility.

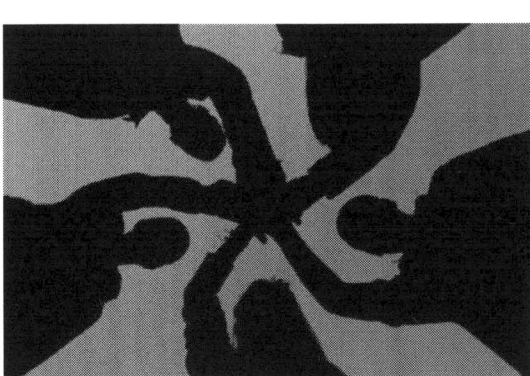

About The Team

We open each chapter with a list of professionals you might need to engage for certain aspects of your financial planning. No advisor knows everything about everything…you need a team to cover all aspects of the financial planning process.

Some team members may be able to cover more than one area. For example, some CFP® (CERTIFIED FINANCIAL PLANNER® professionals) and ChFC (Chartered Financial Consultants) are securities licensed to assist with your investments; some are insurance licensed to offer risk management planning products—or you may need to consult with a CLU (Chartered Life Underwriter) for life insurance advice; some CPA's (Certified Public Accounts) have obtained CFP® or ChFC credentials and therefore are qualified to help you with both tax planning and financial plan construction.

A good financial advisor will be able to provide general information about estate planning concepts, but you need an attorney to actually write wills, trusts, and financial powers of attorney; and perhaps assist with setting up Transfer On Death deeds for your home and other real estate holdings (to avoid probate...more on that in the Estate Planning section).

WHAT TO LOOK FOR IN A FINANCIAL ADVISOR

1. Fiduciary

Investment Advisor Representatives (IAR's), who are required to be registered with the Securities Exchange Commission or SEC, are held *by law* to a "fiduciary" standard for the financial advisory services or advice they provide.

This is a strict standard of care which requires the advisor to put their clients' best interests above their own at all times, with undivided loyalty.

An advisor who only has an insurance license, not a securities license, who may offer insurance-based investment products, is *not* held to a fiduciary standard under law.

That doesn't mean any given insurance professional won't act in your best interest—of course many of them are ethical and do take a fiduciary approach because it's the right thing to do—but they are not *legally* required to act as a fiduciary. Instead they are held to a lower "suitability" standard for each sale of an investment, which means the product should fit the needs of the client at the time of the sale.

"Fiduciary" and "suitability" may seem similar, but the fiduciary standard sets a much higher bar.

First, a fiduciary must disclose conflicts of interest. For example if the company they work for benefits more financially from the sale of one recommended product over another, they need to tell you that. The lower "suitability" standard does not require such disclosure.

A fiduciary is also held to a "duty of care" standard…meaning they must provide ongoing monitoring after implementing a course of action, and help you adjust your strategy over time as your circumstances change. Under the suitability standard, once the transaction is completed, the advisor has no further obligation to care for the client at all.

Some holders of professional designations such as the CFP® and CPA must pledge to operate under a fiduciary standard or risk losing their designation…which is a very big deal to anyone who spent significant time and effort to attain those marks, and whose livelihood may depend on maintaining them. And again, if your planning professional is also licensed with the SEC as an Investment Advisor

Representative, they are held to a fiduciary standard by law whenever they recommend market investments.

Attorneys and others who act on another person's behalf may also be held to a legal fiduciary standard, for example an executor of a will; trustee of a trust, bankruptcy, or other legal entity or process; legal guardian or conservator; real estate broker; company retirement plan administrator; and others.

Always do your homework when you engage with a professional to manage important affairs in your life, and seek someone with a legal fiduciary obligation whenever possible.

2. Designations

Those initials after your advisor's name actually do mean something...in some cases.

But there are those who call themselves advisors who may not have sufficient education and/or experience to give you the guidance you may really need. In fact some "designations" are merely a word soup invented out of thin air to create a sheen of legitimacy. Here's how it works: pick a word from this list...

> Certified
> Registered
> Chartered

...then add one from this list:

> Elder
> Retirement
> Investment
> Financial

...and one of these:

Advisor
Consultant
Coach

...and you too can be a CEC (Certified Elder Coach), CRA (Chartered Retirement Advisor), or RIC (Registered Investment Consultant).

Take time to research the initials behind the name of the person you're entrusting with the planning of your financial future, find out what they stand for, and more importantly find out what is required to earn the right to use them. Start with an online search as if you're interested in attaining the designation yourself—most providers will include on their website the cost, education and testing requirements, experience requirements and other criteria, and areas of study—and many will also estimate the amount of time needed to master the material. This may tell you all you need to know about the relative worth (or lack thereof) of the credentials of an advisor you're considering.

©Daniel Baxter

"Top of the line" financial advisory designations include CFP® (Certified Financial Planner practitioner) and ChFC (Charted Financial Consultant). These each require about 2,000 hours of intensive study, extensive testing, field experience building financial plans for clients, ethics requirements including a background check—and documented continuing education studies to maintain status.

Other top designations include (but are not necessarily limited to) CLU (Chartered Life Underwriter for life insurance), CPA (Certified Public Accountant), CEBC (Certified Employee Benefits Specialist), EA (Enrolled Agent for tax preparation), CPCU (Chartered Property Casualty Underwriter), RHU (Registered Health Underwriter), and CFA (Chartered Financial Analyst, an investment specialist designation primarily for corporate-level industry professionals).

Other common designations require a couple of evenings or a couple of weeks of study, perhaps a few hundred dollars for the price of admission, and little if any continuing education.

Some designations are not frequently seen in the financial services industry but may be relevant or even highly desirable. The PHR (Professional In Human Resources) and SPHR (Senior Professional In Human Resources) designations may indicate expertise and experience in employer retirement plan administration...a potentially helpful characteristic for a financial planner when it comes to facilitating the transfer and management of your 401(k) or 403(b) rollover.

Some accountants, and other specialists, have taken the next step to more comprehensive financial planning services. And more knowledge and experience in any related field may make an advisor a more valuable member of your team.

3. Ethics

Protect yourself from unethical advisors by insisting your advisor's professional designation include ethics requirements that are specific, detailed, and stringent. For most financial professional designations, violation of their governing body's ethical principles may result in suspension or revocation of the right to use the designations, which could be career suicide. The following principals happen to be based on the CFP® code of ethics, but could apply to any line of work that involves an advisory relationship...your doctor, your kids' teachers, and your plumber should operate within these same ethical principles.

Integrity: This is the granddaddy of ethics, and incorporates all the other principals we live by. It's about doing the right thing, even when nobody is watching, by putting the interests of the client ahead of the advisor's own personal gain in *every* situation.

This is a big deal. A good advisor understands that they can make an honest living by being honest. The price for behaving otherwise is lost business and lost reputation, and we believe life is actually easier and better when we do right by clients. How do you know if an advisor operates with integrity and honesty? Start with checking their credentials with their industry regulatory body—for investment advisors it's FINRA.org (the Financial Industry Regulatory Authority) and the "ADV brochure" your advisor should provide you. There you should be able to see a history of formal complaints...or an absence of complaints.

Objectivity: This is another facet of integrity...being impartial and intellectually honest; being able to step outside of oneself to say, "If the greatest advisor in the world was standing here, how would they see this situation?" We think this is also why folks come to us for a second opinion: they (and maybe their current advisor) have been in the middle of their situation so long, they want to know if maybe they're missing something "hiding in plain sight." It happens.

Competence: Advisors are rightly expected to know a lot and to stay on top of new developments in their area of practice. This requires continuing education to maintain their savvy (and their designations, incidentally)—and of course ongoing real-world experience. How do you know if an advisor is competent? The starting point is doing your homework to understand the initials after their name. Some require a lot of study, and if they've passed the exams and are fulfilling their ongoing education requirements, this bodes well for their competence. Other designations, not so much.

Fairness: At its root this is the Golden Rule—treating others as you'd like to be treated; recognizing when you may have a conflict of interest, and disclosing it to the client. Again, this requires a degree of objectivity, and a sense of integrity. If you're getting the idea that these all play into one another, you're right; it's the whole package wrapped in honesty, fairness, and good judgment.

Confidentiality: This is pretty simple—what happens in your advisor's office should stay in your advisor's office. Only those with a "need to know" should know your business. This is a fundamental expectation you should have of your advisor, and any breach of that may be taken as a sign of other potential problems.

Professionalism: this is one of those things that may be hard to define, but you know it when you see it. It's about behaving in a dignified and respectful manner with clients, other professionals, the mail carrier, everyone. Our reputation depends on this. (This doesn't mean we can't share a joke, we love jokes.)

Diligence: this is about paying attention, providing service in a timely manner, being thorough—doing what it takes to avoid dropping any balls. This is your financial life, and your advisor should take that as seriously as your doctor takes their responsibility to your physical health, with great attention to detail. It is an awesome responsibility.

4. Communication Style And Compatibility

The advisor-client relationship should be comfortable for both parties. We make every effort to connect on a real human level with each and every client and potential client.

Communication is key. A common reason folks come to us for a second opinion—and many end up engaging with us—is that we put a big focus on simple, clear communication. It's surprising to us that not all advisors understand this basic concept. People want clarity regarding their finances, not industry jargon.

Some clients need a little time to warm up at the beginning of each meeting with some small talk, especially in the early stages of a new client-advisor relationship. You want to like your advisor, because you may be spending a good deal of time with them and it should always be a comfortable two-way conversation. Others just want to get right down to business.

Whether one prefers stories, facts, deep dives into data, or just "broad stroke" outlines, not every client will be compatible with every advisor. However, some advisors are pretty good at adapting their style to fit a client's preferred manner of communicating. If your advisor isn't matching up to yours, either explicitly tell them what you need, try to pull them in your direction by setting the pace, or look for someone else.

But compatibility isn't just about how clearly an advisor explains concepts. There's an intangible quality to every relationship, something you can't always put your finger on...you just know it's right, or not. Follow your instincts.

5. Scope

Some clients need a complete rebuild of their financial house. Some just need a room addition. As your advisor we need to know what you want and expect from us. This will change over time along with your circumstances, so you should never be shy about expressing your changing needs.

"Scope" may be seen from the dimensions of both width and depth. "Width" is about the number of financial planning areas needing attention. "Depth" is about the extent to which each of those areas needs to be evaluated and perhaps adjusted.

A good starting point is to jot down exactly why you decided to speak with a financial professional in the first place. If there's a single main concern that drove you to seek assistance, your relationship with your advisor may be limited to that issue to start with. Once that topic of focus is managed to your satisfaction, you may only need to revisit it periodically to assess whether it's still under control...while focusing on other areas that may also need attention.

One of our workshop attendees came to see us after the presentation, and brought his investment statements with him. Sam likes dividend-paying stocks, and had held onto a particular mutual fund for several years despite what seemed to be an extended period of mediocre performance. He kept hoping it would improve, but through good economic times and bad it failed to keep pace with his other holdings.

Our analysis found he was correct about this perception, and we were able to suggest alternatives and help him make a move. He seemed to feel much better about his situation even though this was just one relatively small component of his portfolio.

The "width" of the engagement was quite narrow: it was just about his investments. The "depth" was likewise shallow: his discomfort was with just one fund among several.

As usual we asked if he'd like us to take a look at his broader financial picture—his other investments, his retirement income plan, legacy goals and other accumulation targets, Social Security claiming strategies, etc.—but for now he was all set.

But for many of our new clients there are multiple problems they wish to address, and sometimes this becomes apparent even at our very first meeting as one issue after another comes spilling out. So the scope of the relationship may broaden to include those concerns, and we start prioritizing them in order of importance. For example if there are young children and a single primary income earner in the family, and no life insurance, we believe that that exposure can be critical. Concerns about their asset allocation in their workplace retirement plan are legitimate and should be addressed, but that may not be the main thing keeping them awake at night.

Sometimes more than one item may be addressed simultaneously—maybe the client applies for that much-needed life insurance policy, and while waiting for that process to play out, we go ahead and assess those workplace retirement plan investment options.

But as a general rule it makes sense to take on one challenge at a time. Otherwise you may experience "analysis paralysis"—becoming so overwhelmed with the laundry list of important issues, and the multiple steps required to achieve potential solutions that, ironically, you end up doing little or nothing.

This is one more way an advisor can be of enormous help—to guide the conversation toward determining the first step. So you have your marching orders, and your advisor has theirs, and you feel energized knowing you can follow this one clear path to solve one clear problem. When that's taken care of, the next issue can be conquered with the same energy, and with the sense that you are making real progress, one step at a time.

Whatever the scope of your concerns, your financial advisor should be ready at all times to broaden—or narrow—the focus to meet your planning needs. This may include bringing other professionals onto the team, or changing course as circumstances evolve. Adding a room to your financial house, or tearing down a wall, or starting fresh, begins with understanding where you are now and where you want to be, and determining to what extent you need to engage with professionals.

A good advisor will regularly re-assess your financial picture and change the scope of your engagement as appropriate. Remember Sam? We helped him adjust his investments, and reviewed them on a regular basis. A couple of years later Sam's circumstances changed: now he did need help with some other financial planning items, with a new goal of retiring within a specific timeframe. We were there for him (for the planning, and at the retirement party too!).

6. Transparency (Advisor Compensation)

You want to know—and *should* know—how your advisor gets paid. If they're hesitant to tell you this, or the answer is not clear, ask more questions or move on.

There are typically three ways an advisor gets paid for their services: commission, fee only, and "fee-based."

1. **Commission-based advisor compensation:** With this compensation structure, your advisor recommends a product from Company X, you agree to purchase it, and Company X then compensates your advisor directly for using their product. That's a commission. This is the way agents are usually compensated when they offer life insurance, annuities, or other types of insurance products. You don't pay the advisor, the company does. This is not to be confused with commissions in stock and bond trades, which we'll address in the Investing chapter.

   Pros: With insurance products, your advisor's pay doesn't come out of your pocket—at least not directly. Every dollar you put in the annuity or life insurance policy goes to work for you.

   In addition, once the commission is paid to the advisor, there may be no further compensation, as may be the case when for example a client pays an ongoing percentage of their investments under management in a brokerage account. (However there are commission structures which may pay an up-front commission and then an additional amount for one or more years following.)

Cons: While compensation is paid directly to the advisor by the company offering the product, and doesn't come directly out of your account, that money has to come from somewhere, right?

Well it comes out of the insurance company's profits…but where do those profits come from? They come from you and all the other customers. Agent commissions are part of the cost of doing business for the insurance companies, just like their other overhead costs for marketing, accountants, product designers, customer service centers, buildings and receptionists.

All of those costs, including agent commissions, are baked into the premiums (monthly, quarterly, or yearly payments) for life insurance; with annuities, the costs may be recouped via a lower interest rate for you; or lower income payouts for clients with income riders; lower caps on indexed annuities, etc..

There's no such thing as a free lunch. In the end, the advisors' pay comes from clients who do business with those companies…just indirectly.

Now that doesn't mean a commission paid to your advisor is a bad thing—if the product you purchased is a good fit. The agent has to stay on top of those products in the marketplace, screen them to find the one with features that fit your situation; then explain it to you, act as liaison between you and the company, process the paperwork, make the transfers happen—*and* provide service after the sale, meet with you to review performance, help you turn on the income rider when it's time, answer questions. So the agent should make a living for doing all that work, right?

Sure. But what if one company pays advisors 4.5% commission on their product, and another company pays 6%? On a $250,000 investment, that's the difference between the advisor making $11,250, or $15,000. Which product might the advisor be more likely to present to you?

If they're ethical, of course they'll present the product that is the best fit. But what if it's a close call? Advisors are only human, right?

That's why commission-based compensation can potentially present ethical challenges for advisors. This makes it especially important to establish a trust by thoroughly evaluating your advisor and checking their background.

A bigger problem may arise when commissions are the *only* way an advisor gets paid—for example if they are only insurance licensed and not securities licensed.

Their business is completely transaction-driven: if they don't continually make sales, their bills don't get paid. The only products they *can* show you are non-securities; therefore, in the vast majority of cases they will only be able discuss commissioned products. That may be a good fit for part of your portfolio, but how much? For the commissioned salesperson, the more the better—better for them, but not necessarily better for you.

Even with stock market investments, commissions earned from sales or purchases of stocks and bonds may create the temptation to trade excessively (known as "churning"). In our chapter on investing, you'll learn why we believe the fewer trades the better, and not just because of the commissions.

2. **"Fee only" advisor compensation:** This may take several forms. One version works like this: your advisor recommends a market investment (stocks, bonds, etc.) for part of your portfolio; then a percentage of those "assets under management" are paid to the advisor—directly out of your assets—on an ongoing basis.

   Another version involves a consulting fee which may be billed hourly, or on a per-meeting basis, or based on some other timeframe. It also could be a flat fee for the consulting work done regardless of the amount of time it takes. Either way, the advisor is getting paid directly out of your assets (unlike a commission structure).

   Pros: With a fee-only structure, the advisor gets paid the same regardless of which investments or financial planning products they advise. Theoretically this should remove the temptation to push you toward products that are more in their interest than yours.

   Cons: With per-hour or per-meeting compensation, an unethical advisor could be motivated to stretch out the time, or create more meetings than necessary. This may not be easy to spot. You do want the advisor to be thorough, answer your questions, show you more than one option if appropriate, and take the time to get it right. Consulting often involves presenting two or three options, showing the pros and cons of each, and perhaps recommending one of the options over the others.

   Fee-only compensation for advisors does *not* remove the motivation for the advisor to engage with you in the first place...and get your money under *their* management. Step one in the planning process should be to assess your goals and your current situation to see if you need to make any changes at all.

It's also important to note that with an advisor receiving a percentage of assets under management, if the investments grow, the advisor makes more money.

This sounds great at first blush, as it would appear to be in the advisor's interest to get a better rate of growth on your investments, which is what you want...and it *is* in the advisor's interest to get that growth.

But during some periods the stock and bond markets *don't* grow...to the contrary, sometimes your statement balance will be lower than the previous statement due to normal market fluctuations.

One of our clients, we'll call her Mrs. C, is a very conservative investor, but she wanted better growth potential than bank savings, with full liquidity (access to the money with no "excess withdrawal" penalties). So we invested her savings in a conservative bond allocation which historically had performed at about double the current interest rate of bank CD's.

However even bond markets do retract sometimes...nowhere near as badly as a stock market recession, and usually for a much shorter period. This happened soon after our client opened her account with us.

She called us and complained that her account statement showed advisor fees being deducted that quarter, even though the account was a bit lower than before. She said, "You're making more money than I am!"

That stung, because of course we know that's not what clients want to see, and neither do we.

We explained that it's actually *illegal* for an advisor to be compensated as a percentage of the *growth* of her account.

Why? Because back in the days when this was allowed, some advisors used speculative, extremely risky investments contrary to the risk tolerance of their clients, in order to make more money for themselves as a percentage of that extra potential growth.

Under current rules, your advisor is compensated the same percentage of your assets under their management whether the account grows or not. That can certainly be irritating during market downturns…but regulatory agencies believe this reduces the temptation for advisors to engage in risky speculative investing with client accounts.

Mrs. C still wasn't thrilled, but she understood. (And before long the bond markets bounced back as usual).

Of course none of this prevents incompetent advisors from attempting to time markets or pick stocks, in the mistaken belief that this will give you better growth, and therefore increase the dollar amount the advisor receives as a percentage of your assets. Watch for excessive trading activity in your account, known as churning.

3. **"Fee-based" advisor compensation:** The "fee-based" advisor compensation model may involve any or all of the following:

    - An up-front or recurring consulting fee for building a financial plan.

    - 12b-1 fees on investments. For A-share mutual funds for example, that would mean a 3% - 5.75% "front-end sales load" which comes out of your investment, plus an ongoing "trail" often in the 0.25% per-year range; for C-share mutual funds, there's no front-end sales charge but instead a higher ongoing trail typically in the 1% range—again, deducted from your investments.

This is similar to the version of the fee-only structure where the advisor is paid a percentage of your assets—but in that case, there is normally not an additional up-front charge as with A-shares.

- A "fee-based" planner may also use some commissioned products within your portfolio.

Pros: A-share mutual funds may be less expensive in the long run than either C-shares or the fee-only structure.

For example, let's say you pay 5.75% up front sales charge, and .25% ongoing for an A-share mutual fund.

In ten years, on a $100,000 investment you will have paid $5,750 up front, then $250 per year, for a total of $8,250.

With a 1% flat fee, or a hypothetical C-share fund charging 1% more in 12b-1 fees than A-shares, you'd pay $10,000 over ten years.

This example results in a lower long-term cost…but this may only get you the investment, and perhaps not the broader financial planning guidance you may need in addition to investment advice.

A fee-based advisor may offer commissioned products in addition to traditional investments…and this may be a good thing if the product really does fit your needs. In most cases the advisor can't choose an alternative compensation method—the companies set those up.

Cons: If you purchase an A-share mutual fund, you can swap for other funds within the same family (company) without incurring additional front-end loads. However if you decide to change to a different mutual fund company, you would be out a new front-end charge. This could potentially mean less investment flexibility.

Also, many "fee-based" planners may *only* be licensed to offer 12b-1 compensated mutual fund products for the stock and bond market portion of your portfolio—again potentially limiting your investment options.

Finally, we've seen cases where an advisor is charging a "wrap fee" (percentage of assets under management) in addition to receiving ongoing 12b-1 fees...essentially double dipping. This is not common, but you want to make sure it's not happening in your accounts.

Advisor Hazards

There are many ways an advisor can cause more harm than good, but most can be boiled down to:

- Lack of integrity
- Lack of transparency
- Incompetence
- Incompatibility
- Price

You'll recognize some of these from the ethics section; others relate to advisor compensation issues also discussed previously.

Most are under the control of the advisor to one degree or another, but compatibility issues may just be a matter of personality fit. This is a gut check, and like many things in life, you should follow your instincts in this area.

As for competence and integrity: you should have already reviewed the qualifications and experience of any advisor with whom you're considering engaging, including checking with the regulatory body responsible for publically reporting complaints or disciplinary actions (for example BrokerCheck at https://BrokerCheck.FINRA.org). If the advisor is not under the jurisdiction of any such body…well that in itself should give you pause, and there are probably plenty of other qualified advisors in your geographical area (CFP® professionals and ChFC designees for example).

A lack of complaints or disciplinary actions is no guarantee of competence, integrity, or fair pricing, but it's a good sign…and you should know right now if your advisor has been transparent with you (disclosing their compensation)—and now that you understand various advisor compensation structures, you should be able to determine if your advisor's pricing is fair.

If you're not 100% confident in your advisor, make a move.

A Word About Independent vs. "Captive" Advisors

If you need guidance to find your way around the financial services "supermarket," you have two choices: an independent advisor, or a captive advisor.

A captive advisor works for a particular vendor which carries a very specific line of products, sometimes based on rewards received from the product manufacturers.

An independent advisor, on the other hand, can shop across product lines, and research the universe of manufacturers, which can potentially improve your odds of finding a better fit for your needs.

For example, if you want corporate bonds for income, a captive advisor may be limited to those bonds already "on the shelf," perhaps overstocked, and the advisor may be directed by their employer to try to sell those bonds first.

An independent advisor doesn't have to worry about someone telling them what product to "move"—they research the bond market, and simply try to find the bonds that have the quality, duration, interest rate, and other features that fit your circumstances.

That's not to say a captive advisor is a bad advisor, or that the products they recommend won't meet your needs. It's just a matter of degree, and all things being equal, an independent advisor may have a better chance of finding products that fulfill your needs more effectively.

THE PLANNING PROCESS

1. Goal Setting

Your advisor should start with understanding where you are now, and where you want to be. We ask both new and existing clients many or all of the following questions to help clarify goals:

- Tell us about your family...and what are your long-term goals for your family?

- Tell us about your job; tell us about your spouse's job. What are your long-term goals for your careers?

- What leisure activities do you enjoy? Are there others you'd like to do now or in the future?

- Are there civic, charitable, or church organizations you want to consider in your planning? For example do you wish to leave money to an organization as part of your estate and legacy planning? Or maybe you just want to make volunteer work part of your lifestyle now, or in retirement, or both?

- What are you most worried about right now?

- Imagine we're sitting here again three years from now: what would need to have happened between now and then for you to be happy with your progress, both personally and professionally?

- What roadblocks stand in the way of achieving your goals? What are the most important actions you must take to overcome those roadblocks? What do you need to do first?

- When do you see yourself retiring? Have you determined how much money you'll need through retirement? How did you calculate that? Did you account for inflation? Are you on track? What concerns do you have about your retirement savings?

- What else do we need to know in order to understand your current situation and your goals for the future?

We may also ask prospective clients whether or not the following items are of concern:

- Trying to reduce the level of risk in their investments—or attempting to protect their investments from any loss at all.

- Taking steps to improve their potential income longevity, or finding ways to create more income.

- Funding long-term care (nursing home care, assisted living, or anything in between) for themselves or loved ones.

- Understanding and potentially improving their tax situation. (Note: we are not accountants, so we don't offer tax advice, and neither does our brokerage firm…but we can speak in general terms about tax concepts and help clients understand the basics. We can also refer clients to competent local professionals.)

- Legacy issues: for example helping grandkids with college (or a favorite charity) after they're gone.

During this part of the financial planning process, we try not to get sidetracked with a discussion of how to help the client get from where they are now to where they want to be. That conversation will come soon enough—right now we just want to bring clarity to the big picture, the future our clients earned…the fiscal house they are ready to build with our help.

That clarity may not even exist for you yet, so by asking these questions we may help bring your future into sharper focus.

Next it's time to evaluate any planning you may have already done.

2. The Initial Inspection: What's In The Junk Drawer?

Once we understand where you'd like to be, we examine whether your current path may get you there. This means analyzing what you're doing to see what's working well, and where there might be concerns.

Everyone has a "junk drawer" at home where miscellaneous

item gather over time, until that day when it becomes difficult to close the drawer. At some point you have to take a closer look at what's in there—including items in the back you haven't looked at lately, or may have forgotten about entirely.

Some of the things in your junk drawer may still be useful. Some may not.

When we look at your current financial picture, we examine whether each product you own does or does not constructively move you closer to your goals, and to what degree. There are cases where we say, "Congratulations, there's nothing in your portfolio you don't need, and there's nothing missing that you do need, as far as we can see."

Other times there's plenty missing…and some things to toss out.

3. Developing Recommendations

Once your advisor understands your goals and has examined your current plan to see what makes sense to keep—and what needs to be modified, enhanced, or replaced—it's time to build specific recommendations for moving forward.

We believe a good advisor should be familiar with a broad range of financial planning products that can address the major areas of your financial life.

As we've mentioned elsewhere, the financial services industry can be seen as a huge supermarket—but instead of the frozen foods section, or the bread aisle, you and your advisor are shopping in the "income" department, the "risk management" aisle, "investments," "long-term care," and "estate and legacy planning" sections.

Once you find the right aisle and the right product type for your situation, picking a specific brand may simply be a matter of checking the label to make sure the ingredients are healthy, and the price is fair.

Your advisor should evaluate each goal, think about which types of products fit your risk tolerance—and your time horizon, sources of income, and investable assets, as well as your debt and budget picture—and then your advisor should step back and look at the big picture before narrowing down the choices.

The goal is to make sure the jigsaw puzzle comes together correctly to create the picture you described. Getting a client to accurately describe the future they've always imagined is tricky, and making that picture come to life requires broad knowledge, experience, and a special kind of imagination itself.

Every client brings a particular set of specifications to the table, so no two plans are exactly the same. It's a set of math problems, and personality profiles, past experiences that have made a client who they are today…all their fears, hopes, and dreams arising from real-life moments that brought them from where they started as kids to that table in our office where the magic happens.

Developing recommendations for your financial plan is often done between meetings; the next thing you see is the presentation of the plan.

This may take several forms—your advisor may sketch out the overall plan in broad strokes and then suggest starting with the most pressing need or concern. And by that, we mean *your* biggest concern.

In a true consulting relationship, a good advisor may present more than one option for solving a particular planning issue, discuss the pros and cons of each option, and then recommend the path that appears to be most feasible or potentially most effective.

Ask questions until you understand what the advisor is suggesting you do. If you don't understand it, don't do it.

4. Implementing The Plan

So your advisor has learned about your goals and concerns and has developed a strategy to get you there. The rest is a matter of pulling the levers so the planning products your advisor recommended are set into motion in a timely and well-integrated manner.

Typically your advisor (or perhaps their staff) will ask the questions on product applications and ask for your signature. **It is critical that you ask any remaining (or new) questions now so that you are clear on how each piece fits into the overall financial plan.**

Your advisor or their staff should keep you posted on progress periodically as applications are processed by companies providing your financial products.

Keep the ball rolling on your planning items as you have prioritized them with your advisor. The idea is to continue progress without becoming overwhelmed with meetings and information. This is different for everyone, and your advisor should be respectful of the pace that is comfortable for you...while making sure the next step, and its timing, is on pace to meet your planning goals.

5. Monitoring Progress, And Reviews

Checking the progress of your financial plan is especially critical in the first year or so with a new advisor or with a new or expanded plan. Our newer clients may have a number of items to tackle in their "floor plan," in some cases requiring

coordination with their attorney and/or accountant, and it's important to manage those new initiatives carefully.

In some cases there may be a series of weekly or bi-weekly meetings in the early stages, followed by quarterly review meetings the first year to ensure all is going as projected. With simpler planning situations, fewer meetings may be required. However if an advisor is brand-new to you, more frequent meetings may still be preferable until you have attained a sufficient level of comfort. You're the boss.

Once most or all aspects of a new financial plan have been implemented, the ongoing monitoring and review process may be less time-intensive, and meetings may eventually only be needed semi-annually or annually. Review meetings should focus on these areas:

- Progress toward goals: are you on track, or not? Can you (and do you want to) potentially meet your goals with less aggressive investments because of better-than-projected performance, or do you want to apply the surplus to other goals?

- Change of goals, or new goals that need attention.

- Performance of investments, life insurance cash value, etc..

    There are two considerations here:

    1) Is the performance consistent with benchmarks or relevant performance standards for the particular product or investment, under current economic conditions?

    2) Is the performance adequate to meet your short-, mid-, and long-term goals?

- Life changes that may affect the financial plan: new family members, job changes, unexpected changes to your resources—for example an inheritance or unexpected large expense.

- Changes in personal data (contact information, etc.)

Special Planning Considerations For Couples

If one member of a couple has a closer relationship with an advisor, could this become a problem if one or the other dies? Likewise, if one handles most or all of the finances, and the other has no clue: what will happen if the "bookkeeper" dies or becomes disabled?

Talk about this together now, share information, and have a plan in place for a smooth transition in case of tragedy—when life will be plenty upside-down without the added problem of financial disarray.

A lovely couple we'll call Mr. and Mrs. N engaged with us for help with some of their investments...proceeds from the sale of real estate in North Dakota which Mr. N had inherited from his father. His dad had purchased this land many years prior, so Federal capital gains tax was going to be considerable. We talked about strategies to stretch that tax hit over a couple of years, and how to conservatively invest the money so that it would be fairly stable, and available to pay the tax bill the following year.

We came up with solutions, and near the end of the meeting we asked Mr. N if he had any more questions. We turned to Mrs. N and asked the same question; she responded, "I just hope I die first."

Mrs. N didn't feel she understood everything well enough...Mr. N handled most of the finances, and she just felt lost.

From then on we tried to take a little extra time each meeting, addressing one issue at a time, so Mrs. N could catch up, and keep up...so she didn't have to feel so exposed. We're the advisors, and the advice needs to be clear for all interested parties. And she was certainly an interested party.

70% of women change advisors after the death of their spouse…often because they felt ignored or under-informed to one degree or another within the client-advisor relationship, and also in many cases because their spouse handled most or all of the finances and did not create a basic contingency plan for an unexpected transition. [2012 Ruth Ackerman, Investment News, Women & investing: Why Many Advisers Are Missing Out.]

If both members of a couple are not 100% comfortable with the relationship with an advisor, either examine why and fix the problems, or seek a new advisor who is a better fit. Get started *now* on organizing and understanding the roles each of you play in your financial life, as well as each member of your financial team.

There should be specific actions taken in case of death or disability, and you should sketch those out now. If you wait until this becomes a reality, it's too late!

This is about you and your partner knowing your resources and team members: accountant, attorney, investment advisor, financial advisor, insurance agents. Meet every member of the team if you haven't already. Attend reviews. Get a working knowledge of what you own, and how it's protected. Understand the plan for managing assets to meet basic goals. How would the goals change in the event of death or incapacity of *either* of you?

Getting Your Financial Act Together (Not Just For Couples)

Here's a quote from Albert Einstein: "If a cluttered desk is a sign of a cluttered mind…then what about an *empty* desk?"

(Another alleged quote from Einstein: "I never said half the things I'm quoted as saying.")

Does this desk look anything like yours at home? So if the Einstein who takes care of your household finances dies, and this is their desk, what is the surviving spouse or family going to have to do within the next few days and weeks?

If you're the one handling the finances and bookkeeping, we're not saying you have to transform yourself into a neat freak. But will the first question your survivors ask be, "Where *is* everything?"

We offer our clients an organizational tool we call the "Survivors Guide," but you can create something similar yourself using a three-ring binder. It's great for couples as well as individuals.

The centerpiece is essentially a table of contents for your financial life—your personal information, contact information for your insurance agents, stockbroker, attorney, accountant and other advisors, where your assets are located, where the car and home titles are kept, safe deposit box location, bank information (*not* account numbers and Social Security numbers because you don't want those laying around the house—but the secure location where these can be found).

We also include a tab for copies (not originals) of wills and trusts, insurance policies, health care directive, powers of attorney, tax information (again, no Social Security numbers or other personally identifying information), and real estate deeds.

We even include a place to write your own obituary and eulogy so you truly get the last word!

Now it doesn't take an Einstein to come up with something like this. But it's a great guide, a checklist of items you need to organize…and in addition to helping those you leave behind, it can also benefit *you* if you're not already as organized as you'd like to be.

This is not something you complete overnight; it's a project you work on over time. Once it's complete, you can sleep better knowing your survivors can find everything. And maybe it's the surviving spouse who will use this first…if that were to be you, do you already know where everything is? If you helped pull all this information together for your own Survivors Guide, you'd know. And when you do find yourself suddenly on your own, it becomes yours, and you can update it for your own survivors' benefit someday.

And when you show the kids where you keep your Survivors Guide, show them what you did—for them—and ask if maybe they need to organize their own financial lives.

This isn't something we only do for ourselves. We do it for our family, the ones we leave behind to pick up the pieces. This just makes all those pieces easier to find, easier to pick up, at a time when the last thing your survivors want is to have to dig through Einstein's desk.

Special Planning Considerations For Business Owners

An entrepreneur has the same planning needs as everyone else, but with additional considerations critical to helping them grow and protect their company. The legal entity you establish (sole proprietorship, partnership, LLC, S-corporation, etc.) determines your *personal* liability in case of a lawsuit, and your ongoing tax obligations. You can take charge of your own retirement planning destiny if you're selecting your workplace retirement savings plan structure and provider, diversifying your investments—and planning your exit strategy well in advance so you leave the business on your terms, and your timeline, and with as big a payoff as possible. And investing takes on a special twist as you may naturally be over-exposed to a single investment (your business!), so diversification may become more critical than ever.

Risk management and estate planning for business owners is also more complex than for individuals and families. Death, disability, and disaster may threaten day-to-day company operations (and therefore revenue)…and may threaten the very existence of the business itself. Careful contingency planning may dramatically improve your outcome.

An in-depth discussion of business planning and administration is beyond the scope of this book. We offer summary points to consider throughout, but you should seek guidance from professionals who have experience with businesses of your size (and for some planning areas, your particular industry).

2.

Income, Budget, And Accumulation Planning

When I have to break it to a client that they need to earn more, spend less, or seek more investment growth to meet their goals, there's always this pause where they expect me to tell them the other thing they can do instead. Once that passes, we start planning.

-John Piatchek

BOTTOM LINE: Have a detailed written budget; revisit it as often as needed, but at least once per year. Don't overlook "little" expenses that tend to add up.

If your income doesn't meet your basic living expenses, "lifestyle" expenses, debt payments, and your need to save for big-ticket items, then you have three options: increase income, reduce expenses, and/or seek more growth potential for your investments.

Understand how you might be able to accomplish each of these adjustments (review the Investing chapter, including "Income Producing Investments," for starters).

Understand the characteristics of your income sources—consistency, inflation provisions, and tax efficiency—and seek improvement in those attributes for each source.

Take the time to project your expected basic and lifestyle expenses for a comfortable life, and also for a potentially long retirement. Find balance between your current spending needs and the need to save for emergencies, college, retirement, and other big-ticket items. Accumulate those funds in a disciplined manner—by "paying yourself first." Seek tax efficiency.

Understand pros and cons of carrying debt, including the potential arbitrage opportunity of "cheap" (low interest) debt—and the potentially attractive option of becoming debt-free. Know how to manage your debt toward long-term financial success; look for mortgage (or other large debt) refinancing opportunities.

Business owners: a whole book could be (and many have been) devoted to business income, budget, and accumulation planning. But there are many parallels with our discussions of household planning, so look at each concept here in light of both your personal and business planning. Seek more information and guidance from experienced peers and professionals who understand your industry and your unique challenges.

THE TEAM

Almost everyone needs sooner or later:
Financial planning professional
Investment professional (some CFP®, ChFC or other financial planning professionals are qualified for this role).
Accountant

And for some:
>Real estate agent or broker
>Life insurance professional (some use cash value permanent life policy for emergency savings accumulation)

DO-SOME-OF-IT-YOURSELFERS: This part of financial planning is *mostly* do-it-yourself. You are using your limited resources to fund your life…so either you manage your budget, or it manages you. You can adjust your budget, your spending, and your accumulation goals any time by following the basic principles laid out in this chapter.

⌐⌐⌐⌐⌐⌐⌐⌐⌐⌐⌐⌐⌐⌐⌐⌐⌐⌐⌐⌐⌐⌐⌐⌐⌐⌐

How it works in the real world: A woman we met at one of our seminars—we'll call her Mrs. M—came to our office to meet, and asked about an IRA account she and Mr. M had invested. He was a wonderful, once-brilliant man, had always handled the finances but was now suffering from Alzheimer's, no longer able to assist with the investment planning. Mrs. M felt unsure of herself and wanted a second opinion.

She said that one of their accumulation goals was to leave $250,000 to each of their three adult children, and an insurance product salesperson they met a few years ago seemed to have found an easy way to accomplish that.

She said this advisor recommended putting Mr. M's $370,000 IRA into an account that would receive an 8% bonus up front, and then "grow" at a "guaranteed" rate of $72 per day. This would result in a $750,000 account balance within about ten years. Problem solved.

As Mrs. M described this to us, we did a quick calculation to find "$72 per day growth" translated to exactly 6.5% per year added to the bonused principal. But at this time market interest rates were very low, so we knew there was no such thing as 6.5% guaranteed interest.

It looked like Mrs. M had either misunderstood what the advisor had said, or he had misled her—or perhaps it was a little of both.

When we examined Mrs. M's indexed annuity contract, sure enough it included an optional rider which calculated a future guaranteed lifetime income by taking the amount of the original principal plus the 8% bonus, then *only on paper* adding 6.5% per year.

In other words, the *account* wasn't growing at 6.5% at all. The advisor was referring to an artificial "side-calculation" that was used only to determine a future income amount.

We don't know whether the advisor intended to mislead Mr. and Mrs. M. At the very least he failed to make sure his clients were clear on how this investment really worked, and he let them walk away mistakenly believing they would accumulate $750,000 in ten years. For the kids.

To make matters worse, Mr. and Mrs. M didn't need that income rider at all, and there was a fee for the rider which they could not stop and which was hurting the growth potential of the account. So the performance of this investment not only failed to put them on track for meeting their legacy goal, it was *hindering* their progress.

We helped Mrs. M move to more suitable investments over time, and now they are on track. Mr. M would be proud of her for pursuing more information, and making an adjustment to their accumulation strategy.

Even if you find someone you believe to be a trustworthy advisor, it's always okay to seek a second opinion.

Your Budget: Analyzing Expenses

If you haven't carefully tracked your minor expenses lately, do so. Get a clear picture of your spending patterns.

Excessive small convenience and luxuries items like fast food and movie rentals can add up to block your success at meeting bigger long-term goals like retirement savings, major home repairs, replacing your car periodically, or big-ticket wants and dreams.

This is about finding balance between your basics and your lifestyle expenses, and only you can know where that balance lies. Work backward from those big long-term wants and needs—know what they are, know how much of your income needs to be set aside for those each month…and what's *left over* can fund the "little extras."

But regardless of how detailed and sensible your plan, success or failure at fulfilling an income and budget plan (and ultimately your accumulation planning as well), is mostly a function of *your* behavior. You control the spending side of the budget equation with your day-to-day decisions. The income side is also directly affected by your choices over time, as you may take steps to improve your value in the workforce, and thus to some extent create your own destiny.

The "Earn More" Side Of The Budget Equation

If your income doesn't meet your expenses, including the expense of saving for long-term needs, there are just two sides to the equation: either reduce your expenses, or increase your income.

But just saying that reminds us of the old Steve Martin comedy bit: "You can be a millionaire and never pay taxes. Ok. First: get a million dollars…"

Easier said than done!

Earning more may mean getting a raise in your current job, or getting a higher paying job. Are there training and development programs available in your workplace which could get your further down your career path? What about your local career center? Improving your skills and knowledge potentially makes you more valuable to your current employer, and more attractive to other employers if you're willing to make a move for the sake of your long-term financial security.

Increasing your Social Security and/or pension income in retirement is certainly possible with careful planning of your claiming strategy. That's something your advisor may be able to help you with, and we discuss this in the Retirement Planning chapter.

Some investments are designed to be income-generating, or you can simply take capital gains (investment growth) to add to your income—so one way to increase your income is by getting a better growth rate in your investments. We also discuss that in detail in the Investing chapter.

Budget Planning: Basic Living Expenses

See the Budget List at the end of the book for a more thorough checklist, but here are the major categories:

Budget basics include food, clothing, shelter (and all that goes with it—home maintenance, utilities, mortgage payments, etc.), transportation (including gas, maintenance, repairs, parking, etc.), phone and other communication expenses, medical care, and the category we cleverly label "other": those unusual budget items particular to your situation.

If you look at the funding for these expenses as a particular segment of your income, you can then think about the characteristics you would prefer for that income. Generally you want it to be:

1. Consistent (in both amount and timing)
2. Inflation-adjusted
3. Tax-efficient if possible

Whether you're thinking about income from a job, from Social Security or a pension, or from invested savings, it's a useful exercise to think about how each income source stacks up against those three considerations—and look for ways to improve.

For example if part of your income is from the growth of your investments and you're aggressively invested in the stock market, the amount of that income may not be consistent, nor will the timing be consistent as markets fluctuate. If markets do well you may consider investment growth a hedge against inflation, but there's no truly direct inflation offset unless you use something like TIPS (Treasury Inflation Protected Securities) which adjust for inflation but are very conservative, and therefore may not generate much income to start with.

And investment growth may or may not be tax efficient depending on whether you're taking short-term capital gains (less than a year's growth) or long-term capital gains (one year's growth or more) which are subject to a lower tax rate during most historical periods—and also depending on your adjusted gross income. (Important: seek professional tax advice for current IRS rules.)

So using investment capital gains for income may be tricky, but may work well for replenishing cash supplies over the long run.

Employment income may be consistent as long as you can hold the job, and annual pay increases may be considered a hedge against inflation. But in most jobs this is not guaranteed...and employment income is certainly not very tax efficient, especially considering FICA (Social Security and Medicare) withholding.

Social Security is consistent, inflation-adjusted, and some or all of it may not be subject to income tax depending on your other income sources.

It may be difficult to check off all three of the characteristics you'd *like* to see in your income sources. So take steps to account for shortcomings—for example maybe consider using municipal bonds in taxable investments to potentially reduce Federal and/or State tax; perhaps evaluate guaranteed income riders available with some annuities that may provide consistency and perhaps optional inflation adjustments (but understand that these guarantees are only as good as the companies making them; most income riders come with a fee; most annuities have surrender periods with substantial penalties for excess withdrawals; some annuities may be subject to stock market risk…and annuities have particular tax characteristics you need to understand—so work closely with your advisor to make sure you're clear on all the pros and cons, and read your prospectus!).

Budget Planning: Lifestyle Expenses

This list could be nearly infinite. We're talking about activities and items that are not necessary to sustain life, but do help you live "the good life." This includes travel, hobbies, "toys," and other fun stuff…again, see the Budget List at the end of the book for examples.

This list also includes activities that create deeper value for ourselves, our loved ones, our community, and the world: volunteer activities and charitable giving. Volunteer work is mostly free; volunteer travel and charitable giving are not free and they require some level of financial planning for a potentially better outcome.

Building a budget around all of these items can help improve your chances that your lifestyle will be what you want. If it becomes clear that your budget can't support all of your needs and wants right now, having all of these items on paper in front of you can make it easier to see which expenses can be reduced or eliminated to rebalance your strategy.

DEBT MANAGEMENT

Make sure any debt you take on is worth it...it's possible to profit from "cheap" (low interest) debt; expensive (high interest) debt should be avoided. Understand your debt picture and how it really affects your current budget, your credit rating, and your long-term financial plans which may include future debt. Deciding how quickly to pay down debt is both a math problem (how do I come out best financially?) and a gut-check (what will help me sleep better at night?).

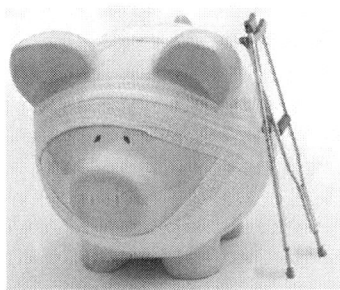

"Cheap Debt" Arbitrage: "Arbitrage" means taking advantage of a price mismatch to make a profit. For example if a local retailer is selling an item on clearance at a 50% discount, but they're going for nearly full price in online auctions, you could buy the item at the store and immediately sell it online for a profit.

A different kind of arbitrage opportunity exists when you can make more money staying in debt than getting out of debt. If you can potentially get 5% growth on an investment (this is hypothetical, not referring to a particular investment!), and you can borrow money at 0%, or 2%, or even 4.9%, you may be able to profit.

Of course there are other costs associated with borrowing and investing money...there may be fees on either end or both ends which can wipe out the difference, or the investing opportunity may change or even disappear...and your time spent researching and implementing such a strategy should be worth something too.

But if your home loan is at a 3% fixed rate, and you can get a guaranteed 4% interest rate on an investment, you can potentially make 1% profit on the money. This is simple math, and it actually works. However life isn't always as simple as the math...read on.

Arbitrage v. Cash Flow: If you take the arbitrage concept to its logical extreme, you would lower your payments all the way to zero on low-interest debt, and instead plow those payments into higher-earning investments.

But in the real world you can't lower your payments to zero. In the real world, minimum payments toward debt are at a level that will eventually pay off the debt. And for every dollar that goes toward paying down the debt, that's one dollar less that's available for your household budget, or to invest.

Even if you can get 0% interest on a credit card transfer, there will be a minimum payment due each month. If you move more and more debt to that "free loan" card, the required monthly payments could reach the point where there's not enough income to keep up with the payments, not to mention all your other budget needs. However if you have surplus income, and plenty of emergency resources, it may make sense to hold some "cheap debt" if some of your assets are growing fast enough to come out ahead.

Finally, always keep one eye on how your debt load could affect your credit rating, and therefore your capacity to borrow in the future—especially if your long-term planning also includes taking on debt, such as a future home or car purchase.

Debt Free By Choice: Sweating The Small Stuff

Regardless of whether you can potentially make more on your money by investing than by paying off lower-interest debt, many people adopt a goal of paying down their debt anyway—simply for the sense of financial freedom this can bring. Once all debt is paid off, the financial picture becomes simpler—*no* income is diverted to debt repayment, so budgeting basic and lifestyle expenses is more straightforward.

However the other extreme—paying down debt with no other considerations—has its own issues. We've all heard you can get debt free and "rich" by eliminating a daily $4 cup of coffee. So yes you *could* eliminate *all* discretionary expenses: no eating out ever, not even a *cheap* cup of coffee, no birthday gifts, no vacations, no fun at all beyond the board games you already own and the "best things in life" that are literally free.

But for many of us, this cure may be worse than the disease. You may *really* like that $4 cup of coffee, and you may make the choice to keep buying it, period.

Years ago a new client and his wife became obsessed with spending less. They kept the thermostat in their home so low during cold weather that they were miserable, sitting on their couch wrapped in blankets…and this was just one symptom of a generally unhealthy lifestyle they had slipped into. They were proud to have gotten out of debt years ago—in fact they now had very substantial assets—but had completely lost the balance required for living the good life.

So if you have too much debt, do consider ways to cut those little luxury expenses: eat out less, maybe have that expensive cup of coffee once per week or twice per month instead of three times per week…because it really does add up. Try giving yourself a set allowance in cash each payday for your "little luxuries" instead of paying for small purchases with a credit card, which is perhaps *too* convenient when you're trying to stick to a budget…when the cash is gone, you have to wait until next payday. This is a way to develop healthier spending habits without cutting off your quality of life completely.

Another mistake some people make is to use tax-advantaged funds to pay off debt, for example raiding an IRA or 401(k) to knock down a loan balance. In some rare situations this *might* be necessary, but you should proceed very carefully to make sure you're not causing yourself more financial harm than good...if the interest expense you save is less than the additional tax hit you cause yourself, it's a losing proposition.

This may be especially true if those withdrawals drive you into a higher tax bracket for the year, or result in a penalty for withdrawals before an IRS-mandated minimum age. The shoe may not drop until tax time the following year, but it may be a heavy shoe.

And you are raiding a pool of money that is intended to fund your retirement, potentially compromising your long-term financial comfort (and tax deferral for retirement savings is a huge gift that should not be sacrificed lightly).

Work with your tax accountant or planner to determine whether or not it makes sense to use such funds to retire debt, and try to find other ways if at all possible.

Debt Free By Choice: Sweat The Big Stuff Too!

Look as closely at your big expenses as your small ones. Housing is the largest expenses for most. But do you have "too much" house? A pricier-than-necessary car? These are not as easy to swap for lower-cost versions, but it can be done if it makes sense...as long as this doesn't needlessly wreck your ability to live a good life, by your own definition of "good."

Debt Management Ratios

If your future includes borrowing money, you need to prepare now.

First, what is your debt ratio? That is the amount of your monthly debt payments divided by your monthly after-tax income, expressed as a percentage. If your payments on houses, cars, and credit cards are more than about 32% of your monthly income, it may be more difficult to get a loan. If it's over about 40%, it may be *very* difficult.

The other critical ratio mortgage lenders look at is the "front-end" or "housing" ratio...they generally want your house payment including principle, interest, taxes, and insurance costs to be no more than about 28% of your monthly income.

These ratios may seem arbitrary, but banks have found from experience that these thresholds are in the ballpark of where the ability of a customer to repay a loan may start running into problems.

To Refinance Or Not To Refinance?

Closing costs for refinancing a home mortgage may vary depending on your circumstances. Figure out how much you'll save if you refinance, and how much of that monthly gain it will take to cover the cost of the refinancing process. If you're not going to be in the home long enough to break even, refinancing may be a bad bet. Take the time to do this math.

But don't simply calculate the savings on the basis of your new monthly mortgage payment if you're stretching your refinance over a longer period than the loan that's being replaced...for example if you had 20 years left on your home loan, and refinanced to a 30-year note, a big part of your reduced payments will be due to stretching the remaining debt over a 50% longer period. Calculate what your new payment would be if you were to pay off the loan in the *same* number of years remaining on the previous loan. This is your true savings from the lower interest rate, and this is the monthly savings which may help offset closing costs:

> **"Real monthly savings" = old mortgage payment minus new mortgage payment** *calculated as if the new mortgage were to be paid off in within same number of years as the old mortgage.*
>
> **New mortgage closing costs divided by "real monthly savings" = months until break-even.**

Other considerations:

- Choose carefully when deciding whether to go with a fixed or adjustable-rate mortgage...this may hinge on whether you can reasonably expect interest rates to drop in the future (and the only time that might be the case is when interest rates are unusually high...and keep in mind you can't know *when* rates may start dropping).

- Understand the long-term effect of paying "discount points" toward refinancing, essentially buying a lower rate which may lower total expenses over the life of the loan, maybe significantly.

- Refinancing in order to fund home upgrades and remodels may not make sense if it means stretching the cost—and racking up the interest payments—over a long period.

Stretch It Out Or Knock It Out?

This comes back to the idea of "cheap debt" creating the opportunity to make more money by staying in debt than by paying off debt. If you're an aggressive investor and can reduce your mortgage interest rate to a point that is lower than what you may potentially get in market growth, you may choose not to pay down the debt any faster than required.

This is not a guaranteed win...the stock market does tend to provide growth potential over the long run, but if the markets don't cooperate in the short-term, mid-term—or potentially even long-term—you may not come out ahead after all. As always, it's okay to consider historical performance, but take it with a grain of salt because past performance *truly* does not guarantee future results.

On the other hand, even short-term "expensive" (high-interest) debt should be employed only when necessary. Long-term expensive debt is almost never a good idea, but may be unavoidable—for example when mortgage interest rates are high and you can't delay taking out a new mortgage. If you have expensive debt, pay it down as quickly as you can comfortably do, and/or refinance to a lower interest rate if possible.

Some proponents of debt-free living suggest paying off small debts first regardless of interest rates, for the emotional payoff you may feel as you rid yourself of a particular large debt sooner.

We can't argue with the psychology of that "positive reinforcement"...but if you understand that the math doesn't support this approach, your psychology may shift on its own. A higher interest rate simply costs you more the longer you let it ride, so the financial math says pay it down first and let lower-interest debt wait.

But if you really prefer the satisfaction of having a lower *number* of loans, despite the monetary savings of paying higher-interest debt first, and this approach motivates you to further improve your financial status, that's fine with us. Sleeping better at night is certainly worth something, and you know better than anyone what helps you sleep at night.

ACCUMULATION PLANNING

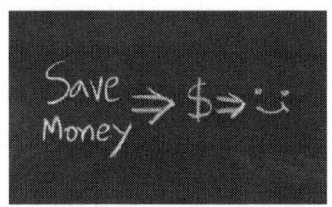

"Accumulation planning" is about building up a fund for items which are above and beyond your basic needs, and too expensive to obtain within one or two paychecks.

Organize your list and "pay yourself first." Have a strategy specifically for emergency savings, and a strategy for retirement savings, and another strategy specifically for your next-biggest (and/or next most important) item on your wish list, and so on.

Adjust the amount and timeline for each item goal until you find a per-paycheck savings goal which your budget can support.

The Wish List

If you're fortunate enough to have cash flow beyond just meeting your basic needs, you can start to prioritize other items that you really want but which are not critical to your survival.

Two special cases are emergency savings, which is a must-have to help protect yourself from financial disaster; and retirement savings, which will be critical to your *comfortable* survival in retirement.

Make a list of your accumulation goals, including your emergency fund and retirement savings. Put the price by each goal, and a time goal (when you want each item).

For each separate item, divide the price by the number of paychecks until your time goal is reached. This is your per-paycheck savings requirement for meeting each goal. Add up all the per-check savings amounts to see the total you need to set aside each paycheck to cover all "wish list" goals. Adjust this amount each time you reach a specific goal.

If the per-paycheck lump sum dollar amount you come up with is too large to reasonably cover each paycheck, either adjust the size of one or more of the individual goals (less expensive car?), or adjust the time goal for one or more of items (buy that car five years from now instead of three years?).

Pay Yourself First

Once you figure out how much you need to save each paycheck to meet your accumulation goals, then start "paying yourself first" each payday. This means setting aside that specific amount each paycheck *before* the money evaporates across all the many small, medium, and large items that can crowd our budgets if we're not careful.

Get in the habit of putting money straight into the bank on payday…or better yet, have it automatically transferred into your savings account on payday. If you don't ever have your hands on the money, you're less likely to miss it (or spend it!).

A special case for emergency fund accumulation may come in the form of a cash value permanent life insurance policy, which may allow withdrawals or loans…however it takes time to build that cash value, so in the early stages focus on simultaneously building your emergency fund with bank savings (paying yourself first).

Earmark Windfalls

Occasionally life tosses us an unexpected monetary win…for example a bonus at work, an inheritance, or a tax refund. (But if your tax refund is large because you had too much withheld from your paychecks, adjust your withholding next year—no sense giving the government an interest-free loan all year just to get a big refund when you could accumulate that money yourself with interest!)

Make a commitment to yourself now to apply any such windfall directly toward your accumulation strategy. Especially this next one...

Emergency Savings Accumulation

There's no financial accumulation goal as important as building a sufficient emergency fund...see our discussion in the Risk Management chapter.

What's the biggest "emergency" expense that you're likely to face? A new roof or heating unit? Learn the estimated lifespan of your current roof or heating unit now, and start saving toward that accumulation goal, on that timeline.

A large medical bill? In a worst-case scenario, how much would it take to cover the insurance copay and/or deductible?

If your income is from working and you lose your job, how long would it take to find new employment, and how much money would you need to get by during that period? What if it takes longer to find new employment than you expected?

So build in some extra cushion. Come up with the *right number for you to be able to sleep at night knowing you're not exposed to disaster—that your emergency savings is sufficient.*

And think about this: what if you actually have to use your emergency savings...how long will it take to build it back up again? What about your exposure during that period? Do you have a low-interest source of borrowed funds to cover emergency needs if you were to find yourself in this position, to cover emergencies while you rebuild your emergency fund? Or can you increase the amount of your emergency savings to cover not only immediate emergencies, but enough extra to cover an emergency replenishment period?

Finally, the "correct" amount of emergency savings may be much less in retirement than during your working years...a common rule of thumb is to have enough to cover a 3-6 month layoff from work so you can cover your basic expenses while finding other employment—but if you're retired and on a reliable fixed income from Social Security, pension, etc., you no longer need that income replacement fund. Adjust your emergency savings target accordingly.

Retirement Savings Accumulation

See the Retirement chapter for this discussion.

College Savings Accumulation

College will likely be one of the biggest accumulation expenses of your life.

Large student loan debt right out of college can be a daunting long-term problem for someone trying to start a career (and perhaps a family); and inflation on college tuition has been historically higher than "regular" inflation for many periods, making it difficult to keep up.

The key to getting ahead of this (or any) accumulation need is to start early.

There are many ways to save for higher education, some of which provide significant tax advantages. Here are the most-used college savings strategies as of this writing:

- **529 College Savings Plans:** These programs are structured within each State, and terms vary so work with an experienced professional.

  A 529 plan lets you save in an investment account on an after-tax basis (sorry no tax deduction), but the *growth* is totally Federal tax-free—that's right, not just tax deferred, but tax-free—as long as the money is spent on qualified college expenses. "Qualified" expenses include tuition, books, class-related fees like computer and lab fees, even room and board (talk to an advisor or see IRS.gov for an updated list of qualified expenses).

  Some plans offer a State tax break as well, some do not; some States give you the break even if you use a plan from another State. Speak with your advisor about options in your own State.

  There is no age limit for the student…and the owner of the account (parents for example) maintain control of the funds regardless of the student's age.

  There is no upper income limit for parents (or anyone else) to be able to contribute.

  However there is an annual limit on contributions from any individual or couple before gift tax becomes a potential issue. Get current information from your tax professional.

  For 529 accounts held by parents, the funds count as part of the "expected family contribution" (EFC) calculation when your student applies for Federal financial aid…but as of this writing the percentage weight applied to it is significantly lower than most other types of savings.

  A 529 plan held by a non-parent is not considered for EFC calculations—but distributions for the beneficiary student are considered a type of income, which may adversely affect student aid the following year.

You must name a beneficiary (student) for the account, but that can be changed to another beneficiary at any time.

Look for plans which offer low-cost investment options, index funds for example, for potentially better performance.

If there is a long timeline before the funds will be used, you may consider using an aggressive stock market allocation for potentially greater growth potential; when college is within five years or so, start reallocating to more conservative investments to help protect against market downturns. See "What Is Your Recession Reserve™?" section of the Investing chapter for a discussion of this strategy for investments in general.

Finally, be sure to let grandparents and other interested family and friends know they're welcome to contribute as well…a great gift for any occasion!

[NOTE: There's no guarantee that a 529 account will grow to cover college expenses. Also, depending upon the laws of your home state or designated beneficiary, favorable state tax treatment or other benefits offered by such home state for investing in 529 college savings plans may be available only if you invest in the home state's 529 college savings plan. Any state-based benefit offered with respect to a particular 529 college savings plan should be one of many appropriately weighted factors to be considered in making an investment decision. You should consult with your financial, tax or other adviser to learn more about how state-based benefits (including any limitations) would apply to your specific circumstances, and you also may wish to contact your home state or any other 529 college savings plan to learn more about features, benefits and limitations of that state's 529 college savings plan. You may also visit www.collegesavings.org for more information.]

- **Coverdell Education Savings Accounts:** These accounts are similar to 529 plans, except (as of this writing):

    o You can't contribute to the plan after the student reaches age 18.

    o There is a lower annual gift-tax-free contribution limit.

    o There is an income limit on parents who participate.

    o Funds must be fully distributed for the student by a certain age (age 30 as of this writing).

    There may be other differences as rules change over time, so make sure you get updated information.

- **Uniform Gifts To Minors Act (UGMA) / Uniform Transfers To Minors Act (UTMA) Accounts:** This approach is not college-specific—funds can be used for any purpose for the benefit of a minor child—but some parents do use these types of accounts for college funding.

    There are fewer tax advantages…and once the child reaches the age of majority (18 or 21 depending on the State), they get control of the funds and may use them for anything they wish.

    For these reasons, most parents now use 529 and/or Coverdell programs for college savings.

The tax advantages for 529 and Coverdell plans disappear if the funds are used for non-college expenses, so don't be tempted to use these accounts for other types of expenditures. Build separate accumulation strategies for non-college basics, wants, and dreams!

Finally, be sure your student visits their school's financial aid office early and often. Scholarships and grants don't have to be paid back, thus potentially reducing the considerable burden of student loans.

Cars And Guitars...And The "Place-keeper"

Here are some possible "big-ticket basics"—expensive items you know you're not going to be able to do without when the time comes:

- Emergency fund
- Car
- New roof for home
- New furnace / air conditioner for home, or other expensive repair/maintenance item
- College (see "College Savings Accumulation" section)

And some possible big-ticket lifestyle items to get you started thinking—start planning now to make your dreams come true!:

- New home or addition
- Big vacations
- Sports car
- Legacy fund (inheritance for your kids or your favorite non-profit perhaps)
- Relocation to (where?) in retirement
- Fancy guitar
- Fancy pool
- Fancy guitar-shaped pool
- Fancy_____

Finally, the "place-keeper": this is the great unknown expense you haven't thought of yet. So get a head start on a dream you haven't yet dreamed, or a big-ticket repair or purchase you can't foresee. It really just amounts to a cushion in your savings goals, and may also come in handy if a basic or lifestyle goal ends up being more expensive than expected. The alternative is to draw from one or more existing lifestyle or basic savings goals, but with a "place-keeper," you can perhaps avoid such a tough decision.

Building Your Legacy

If you're fortunate enough to be able to save sufficiently to cover all of your basic and lifestyle expenses through retirement, and still have surplus money available, you have the luxury of considering what you may leave behind for others someday.

Maybe you want to help fund a grandchild's college education, or set a goal for the amount of inheritance your kids receive.

And maybe there's a church or charity you'd like to support—smaller nonprofits in particular may operate on a thinner margin than you realize, so a bequest at your death could really make a positive difference in the world.

If you have a life insurance policy you no longer need, instead of allowing it to lapse, consider continuing premium payments and making your favorite nonprofit(s) the beneficiary. If you are already making regular donations to a nonprofit anyway, making those premium payments may be a great way to leverage your contributions toward a much bigger result, perhaps even allowing the nonprofit to open an endowment fund that could become a permanent source of cash flow, making your generous legacy gift even more lasting and special.

ᴦᴦᴦᴦᴦᴦᴦᴦᴦᴦᴦᴦᴦᴦᴦᴦᴦᴦᴦᴦᴦᴦᴦᴦᴦᴦ

3.

Risk Management

I don't just tell clients the things they want to hear...I challenge them on the tough decisions needed to protect their families and businesses.

-John Piatchek

BOTTOM LINE: Don't underestimate your odds of facing financial loss due to common hazards that may endanger your life, health, property, income, or even your freedom to stay at home instead of going into a nursing home. And don't overestimate your ability to handle them yourself.

Understand the four ways to manage risk: risk avoidance, risk reduction, sharing risk via insurance, and self-funding losses yourself. Evaluate which of these approaches make sense for each of the common hazards you face.

Seek tax efficiency in your risk management strategies.

Balance costs against benefits when evaluating insurance products.

Review bottom line summaries at the beginning of sections which address "critical risk zones":

> *Emergency Fund*
> *Health Care*
> *Life Insurance*
> *Disability Insurance*
> *Property And Casualty Insurance*
> *Long-Term Care Insurance*

Review your risk management strategies with your planning professionals regularly.

Business owners: seek experienced professionals for contingency planning for your death or disability; key employee death, disability, or resignation; property and casualty hazards including business disruption; and industry-specific liability issues.

THE TEAM

Almost everyone needs sooner or later:
- Financial planning professional
- Life insurance professional
- Property and casualty insurance professional
- Health insurance professional

And in some life stages:
- Medicare supplement agent
- Long-term care insurance professional
- Attorney (if uninsured risks result in legal action)

And for some:
    Disability insurance professional
    Business continuation insurance professional
    Commercial property and casualty insurance agent
    Industry-specific liability insurance agent for some businesses

DO-SOME-OF-IT-YOURSELFERS: You spend every day of your life managing risk...generally by being careful or avoiding risk entirely, or if necessary, paying out of pocket for life's curve balls. Beyond that, you need professional assistance to transfer risk to insurance companies.

How it works in the real world: John recounts the profound experience of paying his very first death claim on a life insurance policy, when he was just twenty-three years old:

"Kevin had recently graduated from college and he wanted some life insurance to help his widowed mother, who he said had scrubbed floors to make a living—and to pay for Kevin's college.

Kevin died in a car wreck a year later.

His mother couldn't stop crying when I delivered that check for $86,000 (in the early 1970's that was still a significant sum). But it wasn't the money she treasured...it was the selfless intentions shown by Kevin's act of love. Through her tears she could only keep saying, 'Thank you, thank you.'

When I think back to that day, I'm reminded once again why we continue to do what we do."

The Four Ways To Manage Risk

Risk comes in many forms, but there are only four ways to take control.

1. **Avoid it.** Don't get in fist fights, don't parachute, rodeo, or walk down dark alleys with money sticking out of your pocket. If you want to be extra careful don't drive or walk down the street at all, don't interact with other humans who may carry disease, and don't own a home or business. (Obviously some hazards are easier to avoid than others!)

2. **Reduce it.** Wear your seat belt and maintain your car's brakes and other safety features; look both ways before crossing the street, make sure your home smoke alarm is in good working order; maintain a healthy lifestyle.

3. **Share it.** Pay monthly or annual (or one-time) premiums to an insurance company who will reimburse you if a risk results in financial loss...this is how property and casualty insurance works, and health, life, disability, and long-term care insurance, and business continuation insurance. An annuity with lifetime income provisions shifts to an insurance company the risk of running out of money in retirement (we'll discuss annuities in the "Investments" section).

4. **Self-fund it.** If the resulting financial loss is relatively low, or "uninsurable," then we have to bear the cost ourselves—just say "that's life," pay the piper, and move on. There's always the risk that we will run over a nail and need to buy a

new tire, but there's not an insurance policy to cover that so we can't really share the risk. The risk may be avoidable (don't drive, and if you do, watch out for nails) or you can reduce the risk (buy tough tires), but in the end we all just understand we may have to buy a new tire occasionally. In fact most risks in life fall into this category...but we're here to talk about the others.

Recognize each of the significant types of risk in your life, and for each of those risks understand your options within the four ways to manage risk.

ΓΓΓΓΓΓΓΓΓΓΓΓΓΓΓΓΓΓΓΓΓΓΓΓΓΓ

RISK MANAGEMENT CRITICAL ZONE I: EMERGENCY FUND

BOTTOM LINE: Make this an absolute top priority in your financial planning—treat it as step 1. Picture events that could cause you to need emergency money, and identify potential sources for those funds right now.

Make sure your emergency fund is liquid (available on short notice), and stable (not subject to significant market volatility). Adjust the size of your emergency fund when your circumstances change.

Have a strategy for rebuilding your emergency fund quickly, or be ready to identify other temporary resources, if you were to actually need to use your emergency fund.

Read the "Emergency Fund" section of the Income, Budget, And Accumulation Planning chapter for a discussion on how to plan, build, and maintain your emergency fund.

An emergency fund falls into the "accept it and bear the cost yourself" category of risk management.

Here are a few reminders of why you need an emergency fund, or at least a plan of action for potential life events:

- You could lose a source of income (job loss, death of a breadwinner, loss of a pension plan).
- You may unexpectedly face an illness or injury with high insurance deductibles, copays or self-funding of out-of-pocket expenses.
- Your roof blows off or the air conditioning unit dies.
- Unexpected major car repairs.
- Unexpected travel expense.
- Family emergency.
- What else?

Think hard about these items, especially the "what else?" placekeeper...the size of your emergency fund depends on it. What is the biggest expense you could face? What if Murphy's Law kicks in, and two or more of these events happen at the same time?

Your emergency fund may also be part of a "share it" strategy, for example if you choose a significantly high deductible on an insurance policy. What are your options if a catastrophic medical loss happens?

If your health insurance has a $10,000 deductible and you have a major injury or illness that uses up the deductible, you have two choices: pay the deductible all at once, or pay it in installments.

Health care providers don't like payment plans on deductibles and other out of pocket expenses but they may accept such an arrangement if necessary, and in some cases this could amount to a "zero interest loan" for you. Weigh that option against the time required to replenish your emergency fund if it's suddenly depleted by a large deductible payment; but also consider the impact on your budget and cash flow if you have to repay a debt over a multi-year period.

Sources of emergency money should be liquid and not subject to significant volatility (fluctuations in value—for example a stock market investment is not a good candidate for an emergency fund!).

Sources Of Emergency Money

Your emergency fund may or may not need to be entirely "same-day" liquid (or should it? Think this through for your own particular potential emergency cash needs), but should at least be available relatively quickly. Here are some options for emergency funds:

- Cash in the bank: a checking or savings account separate from your everyday spending account.

- Home or business equity line of credit, or credit card: perhaps a reliable source and maybe an acceptable method...if you can get a reasonable interest rate *and* your cash flow is sufficient to pay the debt back pretty quickly.

- Cash value in a life insurance policy: this may be a source for emergency funds, *but be very careful here*...make sure your policy won't be adversely affected—including potentially lapsing—if you take a loan or distribution. Some policies are designed for cash value to fund premiums over time, so taking out cash may affect the long-term performance or even the amount of the death benefit in a life insurance policy.

    Talk to your agent or the insurance company to make sure you understand the ramifications of using the cash value in an emergency. And don't forget it may take a few days or more to actually get the money in hand.

- Bond or other stable investment fund: even bond funds may fluctuate in value somewhat, and if for example you have to tap a bond fund during a 2% downturn you will lock in that loss on the amount you withdraw.

However a bond fund could be a good candidate for a "backup" emergency fund in a pinch. Don't forget it may take a number of days to receive these funds from a brokerage account.

An Emergency Fund For Your Emergency Fund?

Don't forget to plan next steps if and when you actually need to use your emergency money. If your surplus cash flow is not sufficient to build your emergency fund back up quickly after a large emergency expenditure, or you don't have some other resource for unexpected expenses while you rebuild your emergency fund, you might consider increasing the size of your emergency budget to begin with.

If your "emergency fund backup" during the emergency fund rebuilding period includes credit cards or a home or business equity line of credit, you'll need to plan for a reduction in cash flow while you make payments.

RISK MANAGEMENT CRITICAL ZONE II: HEALTH CARE

***BOTTOM LINE:** Going without health insurance could be catastrophic to your financial wellness. Consider using tax-advantaged workplace health insurance plans if available, especially if your employer pays some of the premiums. Otherwise, shop annually for coverage that fits both your health care needs and your budget.*

Carefully weigh the balance between the cost of premiums and the cost of deductibles, co-pays, and other out-of-pocket expenses based on past usage and projected near-future needs. A lower deductible may or may not be worth higher premiums.

Consider insurance alternatives and enhancements such as "health care sharing ministries," and tax-advantaged Health Savings Accounts and Flexible Spending Accounts.

Watch for Medicare enrollment deadlines if you're approaching retirement age; get (free) professional assistance shopping for Medicare supplements, and shop again yearly.

According to a 2013 report from the Agency For Healthcare Research And Policy, the average hospital stay costs about $12,500 for people age 45-84…and if your stay is for a heart surgery or liver transplant, the cost may be far more than the cost of your home.

You can't predict when or why you'll wind up in a hospital, or doctor's or dentist's office, so plan to share some of the risk with others by means of private and/or public insurance.

If your workplace offers a health insurance plan, your employer may or may not cover part of the premiums. If they do, the price may be hard to beat; if your spouse's employer also offers coverage, look at costs and coverage levels for both plans…in some cases it may be more cost effective for each of you to get individual coverage rather than "employee plus spouse" with one plan or the other.

If you have multiple provider (doctor) networks in your area, verify the in-network doctor list includes your doctor if that's important to you, as out-of-network copays and deductibles may be much higher.

Another advantage of most employer-sponsored healthcare plans is that the premium payments come out of your paycheck on a pre-tax basis, reducing your payroll tax burden and giving you more take-home pay. If instead you purchase individual coverage on the open market, you can only deduct the premiums which exceed certain IRS-mandated income thresholds. Seek current tax advice from a professional.

If you don't have access to an employer plan, or your employer doesn't share premium costs, there are insurance professionals who can help you shop the retail market. Ask your current life, auto, or homeowner's insurance agent if they can refer you to someone. Getting this kind of help could save you a lot of time and energy, as they know what questions to ask about your health history, expected future needs, etc., to help narrow down a potentially vast number of choices.

Revisit this process every year or at least every couple of years as the marketplace may change significantly.

When Is A High Health Insurance Deductible Better?

While it may seem sensible to choose a plan that covers everything with little or no out-of-pocket expense for you to pay, higher premiums may more than offset that advantage. Insurance companies are in it for the profit, and they price plans accordingly…in general you have to pay one way or the other.

At the other end of the spectrum are plans with high deductibles (and maybe high copays and other out-of-pocket costs) which will tend to have much lower premiums.

Whether you buy insurance through an employer, or in the individual market, figuring out which if any deductible structure is right for you is one of the trickiest aspects of shopping for health insurance. Weigh these factors:

- Cash flow considerations: will your budget allow higher premiums in exchange for a lower deductible? Do you have enough emergency savings to cover a high deductible? You'll need to plan for both ends of this equation.

- How healthy are you? If you rarely need health care services, and have no reason to think that will change, a higher deductible may be the right choice. If you expect to need a lot of services, a lower deductible may make sense. Write a list of services you estimate you'll need over the next year, and in two columns list the cost for each service with a high-deductible plan and with a low-deductible plan. Add everything up and see which comes out more favorably. Again, a professional advisor may be able to do all of this for you more efficiently, and at no extra cost to you.

- Are you willing to put in some extra time and effort as a consumer to shop for the best deal on services, or even haggle with providers for price breaks? If you have a high deductible, it may be worth the trouble.

Some employers offer "high deductible insurance plans," sometimes called "consumer directed health plans" because they tend to cause people to focus more on the actual cost of services, and perhaps shop more carefully. The definition of "high deductible" is very specific in the IRS tax code, and may vary over time. If a high deductible plan is available at your workplace (or if you purchase a high deductible plan on the individual market), you'll also be able to participate in a "Health Savings Account" (HSA)...read on.

Health Savings Account: Quadruple Tax Play

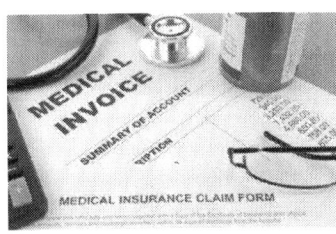

A "Health Savings Account" (HSA) may be available if your employer offers a high deductible health care plan; and even if you purchased such a plan on the individual market, you can take advantage of an HSA. You choose the amount to set aside in the HSA (up to the IRS-defined limit each year), and you can adjust how much you put in each year as your needs and goals change. (Seek current advice from a professional, and if you are a business owner find out if you are allowed to participate under current IRS rules.)

Tax play 1: The HSA allows you to put *pre-tax* money up to defined limits into an HSA at a financial institution (such as a bank). In other words you can deduct contributions from your taxable income, thus reducing your tax burden for the year, and putting that money to work for you instead of Uncle Sam.

Tax play 2: The money grows tax deferred—you don't pay tax on interest, capital gains, or dividends during the growth period, and if you play your cards right…

Tax play 3: The money comes *out* of the account totally tax-free if used for qualified medical expenses. **(IMPORTANT: if you use the money for anything except qualified medical expenses before age 65, you will be subject to a *stiff* penalty in addition to ordinary income tax! Seek professional tax advice.)**

Tax play 4: Any money remaining in your HSA after age 65 can still be used for qualified out-of-pocket medical expenses—and if you decide to use it for other types of expenses, you will no longer be subject to the harsh pre-65 penalty. So from a tax perspective it will behave like an IRA—you will pay ordinary income tax but no penalty. So if you add more to your HSA account than you end up needing for medical expenses, you've still benefitted from the first two tax advantages (deferring income tax and deferring tax on the growth), and may have even boosted your tax-deferred retirement savings above and beyond the limits on IRA, 401(k), and 403(b) accounts by putting additional money in your HSA.

Health Savings Account: IRA Supercharger For Age 65+

As of this writing, the limit for a family HSA contribution is actually higher than the IRA contribution limit...and once you reach an IRS-specified amount of money in your HSA, you can put the money into investments instead of just bank savings, for more growth potential.

And again, after age 65, if you use HSA funds for qualified health care expenses the money comes out completely tax-free; but even for non-medical expenses, you only pay the same income tax as you would if you were drawing from an IRA (with no additional penalty).

So if you've reached your IRA contribution limit and wish you could contribute more for after-65 retirement needs, and you have a health insurance plan that meets the definition of "high deductible" in the tax code, consider maximizing your contributions to your HSA.

Health Care Outside The Box

Do a little research to see if there are alternatives in the marketplace to traditional insurance. For example as of this writing there are "health care sharing ministries" which are not technically health insurance companies but which provide reimbursement for many medical services, including optional catastrophic care in some cases.

Because of the religious affiliation of these entities, members receive an exception to the Affordable Care Act (Obamacare) requirement to purchase traditional health insurance as of this writing. **However there may be important differences in what is covered and what is not covered compared to traditional health insurance. The cost structure may also be very different than traditional insurance; as of this writing, basic membership payments are *not* tax deductible (although additional donations to the organization may be); and there may be other requirements for participation including prohibitions of certain behaviors...so read the fine print**

very carefully.

These special medical cost-sharing organizations may also *require* you to attempt to negotiate with healthcare providers for lower costs. Despite the differences (and for some, *because* of these differences), some of our clients find such cost-sharing "clubs" very attractive from a cost perspective and also for philosophical/spiritual reasons.

We should mention that we became aware of these "new" health sharing ministries during a conversation with a client—yes, there are times advisors and clients can actually learn from each other. So don't be shy about sharing interesting information from outside sources with your own advisor!

Take Some Healthy Tax Breaks

Finally, don't forget to take advantage of any and all opportunities to help reduce your tax burden by deducting expenses related to health care.

If your employer offers a "Flexible Spending Account" program (pre-tax payroll deductions to be used for IRS-approved out of pocket health care *and child care* expenses), participate.

If your out-of-pocket expenses exceed certain thresholds (above a certain percentage of your income), you may be able to deduct those expenses. Work closely with your accountant or tax-preparer to make sure you don't leave money on the Treasury table unnecessarily.

Medicare

The following information is based on our interpretation of Medicare rules as of this writing—seek updated information from a professional who is experienced with Medicare. Information may also be found at Medicare.gov and CMS.gov.

Medicare is public (Federal) health insurance we all pay into in our working years and is available starting at age 65. The government reimburses doctors and hospitals directly for your health services under this system.

You have a limited-time window to enroll around the time you reach age 65. **As of this writing, if you miss this enrollment period you will pay a *10% higher premium* for every twelve months you're late.** "Medicare Part D" for prescriptions also penalizes you with higher premiums if you miss the deadline, and the penalty is added to your premium **not just the year you miss the deadline, but for as long as you have a Part D plan.** Don't let this happen!

Like most other kinds of health insurance, Medicare requires us to pay part of the bill in the form of copays, coinsurance, and deductibles...with no annual limit on those out-of-pocket expenses. If you want more of those expenses to be covered, you have two choices:

1. Purchase a **"Medicare Advantage Plan" (also known as "Part C")** from a private insurer. These plans run parallel to Medicare, and may be seen as a sort of substitute for Medicare...in fact Medicare reimburses these plans with money that would have otherwise gone directly to your health care providers.

   To qualify for these subsidies, insurance companies are required to cover everything Medicare covers except hospice care (which you can still get from Medicare). Some also provide health care services that Medicare doesn't cover—for example, dental and vision services, hearing aids and prescriptions (again "Medicare Part D" is for prescriptions, but may have significant limitations and cost sharing requirements which some Medicare Advantage Plans could help cover).

   The cost of Medicare Advantage plan benefits may vary somewhat from Medicare, within certain limits, and you may be required to use network doctors as with other kinds of health insurance. There are limits on your out-of-pocket expenses, but these limits may vary from provider to provider. This is why we believe it's critical to get professional guidance when shopping for one of these plans (more about that below).

2. Purchase a supplement known as a **"Medigap"** policy from a private insurer. Medigap isn't a substitute for Medicare; instead it enhances Medicare by reducing some of your out-of-pocket expenses. Medigap plans may also cover items not addressed by Medicare, for example emergency health services when traveling abroad. However Medigap plans as of this writing do not cover prescriptions—for that you'll need a Medicare-approved (otherwise known as Medicare Part D) prescription plan.

Here's why Medicare supplements are so important to get right: Medicare only covers about 51% of an average couples' health care in retirement according to 2015 HealthView Services' "Retirement Health Care Costs Data Report."

So an average healthy couple age 65 needs about $395,000 to cover everything through a normal lifespan, even with a Medicare supplement.

Assuming 25 years of remaining lifespan, and assuming your investments grow at 6% (just hypothetically, not referring to any specific investment), you would need to start with about $201,954 of savings at age 65 savings to cover this expense. And Medicare charges higher premiums for people whose earnings in retirement exceed certain thresholds.

So shopping for a Medicare Advantage or Medigap policy and/or a prescription plan—or deciding whether to stick with basic Medicare alone—is critical but can be very complicated. You should consider the potential cost differences and coverage levels, and check what the results would be under each plan option for services you need now or may need over the next year. And here's another twist as of this writing: if you are in a Medicare Advantage plan for more than one year and then decide you want a Medigap policy instead, you will have to "health-qualify" for the Medigap plan. **This means you could potentially be rejected for coverage at that future time, and be stuck with Medicare only—no supplement**—so consider this carefully before making a decision.

And you must review your policies every year: even if your needs don't change, the Medicare Advantage and/or prescription plans themselves could change, potentially costing you dearly.

Our friend Audrey who helps us with Medicare questions tells us about a client whose premiums and copays the current year totaled $1,096; but the following year the client's medication was scheduled to be removed from the formulary ("preferred") prescription list, potentially increasing her expense to $4,700 for the same purchase. Participating network pharmacies can also change, as can the cost-sharing structure of a plan…all resulting in potentially higher costs for you. And doctors sometimes change network affiliation, so if keeping the same doctor is important to you, verify their participation each year.

So each year during your enrollment period (October 15 – December 7 as of this writing), go shopping again.

As if all of that is not complicated enough, there's one more option: the Medicare Medical Savings Account, or "Medicare MSA." This pairs a high-deductible health insurance plan from a private insurance company with a savings account earmarked for medical expenses. There are no premiums to pay; Medicare simply puts a certain amount of money into your health savings account. The catch is, once you spend all the money for that year, you must pay all expenses out of pocket until you fulfill a high deductible. If you fulfill the entire deductible, the plan will cover additional expenses for the rest of the year…and then you start over the next year.

The money you spend out of the medical savings account is not taxable, and unused funds carry over from year to year—making it advantageous to shop carefully for health care services to try to preserve your account balance.

However Medicare MSA plans don't cover Medicare Part D prescriptions.

If your eyes are starting to glaze over...don't worry. Fortunately there are professionals who can walk you through the maze of Medicare-related options to help narrow them down to the best fit for you. In many cases there's no direct cost for this service; however commissions paid to these agents by the provider companies may vary, potentially creating a motivation to steer you toward one company over another. So the same process for finding a trustworthy financial advisor applies to finding an agent to discuss your Medicare options...if possible get a referral from someone you trust.

᠆᠆᠆᠆᠆᠆᠆᠆᠆᠆᠆᠆᠆᠆᠆᠆᠆᠆᠆᠆᠆᠆᠆᠆

RISK MANAGEMENT CRITICAL ZONE III: LIFE INSURANCE

BOTTOM LINE: If you don't need life insurance, you don't need it; if you do need life insurance, you absolutely *need it*—now.

Stop pause to consider what would happen to your household budget and long-term financial plans if one or more breadwinners died today. Imagine the scope and duration of specific financial challenges the survivors will face tomorrow, and the first of next month when bills come due. If there are surviving children, what will be the new expenses for their care? What about major unfunded future expenses: debt, college, cars, major home repairs and medical bills? Retirement? What else?

Know what questions to ask your life insurance agent; participate in the continual re-evaluation of your life insurance needs and the products you're using to meet those needs.

Understand how term life insurance works and the various types of permanent life insurance—some of which build cash value which could fulfill other financial planning goals. Know the tax ramifications of the various available products. Understand the pros and cons of a life insurance "modified endowment contract" (MEC).

Avoid what we call the life insurance "Tax Triangle Of Doom" which makes your life insurance death benefit taxable.

Keep your beneficiaries and contingent beneficiaries updated.

Buy Now!

By purchasing life insurance now, you'll lock in both your age and your health for underwriting (price-setting) purposes, and potentially save yourself and your loved ones a lot of unnecessary additional grief in the long run. You'll never be younger than you are right now—and probably never any healthier either.

Some clients consider waiting to purchase life insurance so they can lose weight, quit smoking, etc. to get a better price.

But if you need life insurance now, you *absolutely* need it now. You can go back to your insurance company (or have an independent agent shop elsewhere) after losing weight or quitting smoking, and request re-underwriting to reduce your premiums—but if you need life insurance now, buy it now.

Uses Of Life Insurance Death Benefit Proceeds

Below is a planning tool we use to help clients clarify their life insurance needs. You may have special considerations—for example business owners may have a special subset of one-time and ongoing needs that may be met by life insurance—but the list below covers the basics for most individuals and families.

How much life insurance do you need?

Final expenses:

Funeral approx. $6,000 (cremation approx. $1,500):	$_____
Other final expense e.g. airfare for family/friends:	$_____
TOTAL FINAL EXPENSES	$_____

One-time expenses:

Home mortgage: pay off? Reduce to lower payment?	$_____
Other debts: loans, credit cards, medical bills, etc.?	$_____
Future or current college costs?	$_____
Emergency fund for survivors? (3-6 month's income?):	$_____
Estate taxes:	$_____
Legacy: charity, grandkids' college, inheritance, etc.	$_____
TOTAL ONE-TIME EXPENSES	$_____

Living expenses for surviving dependents:

Annual living expenses	$_____
Surviving spouse annual income	$_____
EXPENSES MINUS SUVIVING SPOUSE INCOME:	$_____
Number of years needed for living expenses	_____

Est. annual investment growth on life insurance proceeds _____%

LUMP SUM NEEDED TO MEET SURVIVOR LIVING EXPENSES, BASED ON ESTIMATED INVESTMENT GROWTH RATE (requires financial calculator): $_____

TOTAL ONE-TIME EXPENSES
+ LUMP SUM FOR SURVIVOR EXPENSES

$_____

MINUS VALUE OF ASSETS THAT CAN BE SOLD TO CONTRIBUTE TO SURVIVOR NEEDS:

$_____

NET TOTAL LIFE INSURANCE NEED: $_____

You may need help with the "lump sum needed to meet survivor living expenses, based on estimated investment growth rate"—your advisor should be able to assist with their financial calculator or software.

Review this list of needs from the perspective of "spouse A" passing today; then repeat the exercise from the perspective of "spouse B" dying today. The results may be dramatically different; for example, if one spouse earns significantly more than the other, or if one of them is receiving a retirement pension with less than 100% survivor benefit, or a higher Social Security benefit (the survivor receives the equivalent of the largest of the two Social Security checks, not both).

Calculating the amount of life insurance required to meet ongoing needs of survivors may be tricky, as this depends partly on the growth rate of investments used to meet the need. This is where you may need professional advice to find the right balance between liquid cash on hand and invested assets earmarked for future or ongoing needs.

Term Life Insurance: "Renting" Protection

Term life insurance is the "rental plan"...it's only good for a specified period of time, typically ten, fifteen, twenty, or thirty years. After that, the premiums may go through the roof.

Term life insurance may be appropriate for temporary needs: for example retiring a home mortgage if the breadwinner were to die prematurely; or fully funding college for a child if an existing savings plan would fall apart in the event of a death.

Permanent Life Insurance: "Owning" Protection, And A Roth-Like Feature

If term life insurance is like renting, permanent life insurance is owning. As long as you keep paying the required premiums, the policy stays in force.

And with permanent life insurance you may build cash value, explained below. Withdrawals (or loans that you repay to yourself with interest) from life insurance cash value are tax-free **as long as you're not withdrawing more than the total you've paid in**.

This is similar to Roth IRA treatment, where even the growth of your investment can be pulled out tax-free (as long as Roth IRA rules are met...seek professional guidance to understand Roth IRA provisions).

There are two types of permanent life insurance: whole life and universal life.

1. **Whole Life:** regular premiums are paid either throughout the life of the policy, for a specified period (typically ten or twenty years), or even in a single large payment up front (**this may result in a "modified endowment contract" with potential tax consequences—seek professional guidance**).

   The death benefit is guaranteed regardless of how long you live (although with some policies the death benefit is paid out at a certain age, often age 100, even if you're still alive...this is called "endowment").

   Some whole life policies build cash value in a side account via fixed interest, or dividends (profit sharing from the insurance company in a "participating" policy). Cash value may be withdrawn or borrowed **...but be careful: withdrawing cash value without paying it back (plus a specified rate of interest) may result in a lower death benefit.**

   Cash value may also be designated for purchase of additional death benefit.

2. **Universal Life:** these policies offer some flexibility in premium payments and additional options for how cash value attains its growth potential—therefore these policies are generally more popular these days than whole life policies.

   With a universal life policy you can skip payments if you have built up enough cash value to cover them; you may also seek to increase the cash value by adding extra money beyond the required premiums (up to a point—be careful here as there can be tax consequences if you go overboard with adding money or taking money out—work closely with your advisor). Some of our clients use this as an emergency savings account if they need life insurance anyway.

   The cash value provisions for universal life policies are similar to whole life, but with more options for seeking growth of the cash value:

- **Universal Life (UL) with fixed interest rate:** This type of policy specifies a current interest rate, a minimum interest rate, and a maximum interest rate for the cash value component. These rates are generally linked to interest rates in the broader economy, so if banks are paying good interest rates on savings accounts, you'll likely see relatively good rates in universal life policies.

  Interest rates in these policies may vary over time to some degree but the range is contractually limited and changes are usually gradual (although this is not guaranteed).

- **Variable Universal Life (VUL):** Cash value is invested in underlying funds in the stock and bond markets. Cash value growth potential is greatest in this type of policy—but so is market risk, especially if the account is invested aggressively (weighted more toward stock funds than bond funds). If there's an economic recession and stock markets drop, so does your cash value.

  This potential volatility could cause problems if your premiums were determined in the beginning using an overly aggressive cash value growth assumption. For example if your agent plugged in a 10% growth rate assumption on the cash value, this could result in lower premium payments than if they had plugged in a 7.5% growth rate assumption. However if the markets suddenly drop and your growth rate is less than projected for a period of time, you may need to increase your premiums to cover the cost of the life insurance portion of the policy.

  This may be especially troublesome if you stopped paying premiums entirely because you had a lot of cash value built up and believed you wouldn't have to pay premiums ever again.

  It's best not to overestimate growth potential when making a decision to stop paying premiums, and even then, be prepared for the possibility that you'll have to kick in some unexpected premiums down the road if stock and bond markets don't cooperate.

- **Indexed Universal Life (IUL):** Cash value earns interest based on the performance of a stock market index such as the S&P 500 but is not actually in the stock market.

  If the index is down for the year (or other period specified in your policy), your cash value doesn't gain, and it doesn't lose.

  If the index is higher at the end of the specified period, you get part of the gains under a formula such as a "capped" percentage. For example if your cap is 9% and the S&P 500 is up between 0 - 9%, you get all of the gains. If the S&P 500 is up more than 9%, you get 9%. There are other crediting methods but in all cases if the index is down, you don't gain, *but you don't lose previous earnings* as you would in a variable universal life policy.

  This method may give you better growth potential than a fixed-interest-rate Universal Life policy, but you may have some zero-growth years unlike a fixed rate. And it may potentially result in less market-related risk than Variable Universal Life—but you may sacrifice some of the growth potential of Variable Life in exchange for this stability. For some this is a "happy medium."

Again, Universal life policies are more popular now than whole life policies because of the additional flexibility with premium payments, and the extra choices in how growth potential of the cash value is attained. However you may prefer the simplicity of a whole life policy, so discuss the pros and cons (including costs) of these options with an insurance professional to be sure they are right for your needs.

The Permanent Life Insurance Four-Quadrant Win

Permanent life insurance may be significantly more expensive than term life insurance, and not everyone needs permanent insurance. For example if your only need for life insurance is to cover a 15-year mortgage and college for your ten-year-old, a 15-year term policy may be appropriate.

But because some permanent life insurance policies build cash value that you can use while still keeping the life insurance component intact, a permanent policy can fulfill one or all of these four critical areas of financial planning (young families should consider all four):

1. **Life insurance protection for your family.** This one is pretty obvious!

2. **Emergency savings.** Once the cash value account is built up to a sufficient level, it may serve as an emergency fund to cover a large unexpected expense such as a medical deductible or a new roof. **Please note it will normally take several years to build significant cash value. Work with your agent to understand the timeframes involved, and what could derail projections. Always have a ready source of emergency funds!**

3. **Income replacement in case of a disability that knocks you out of work.** This may be in conjunction with disability insurance, as a way to cover the "exclusion period," the waiting period before disability insurance payouts begin—generally the longer the exclusion period, the lower the cost of the disability insurance, so having another pool of funds from which to pull can help you leverage this tradeoff. **But again: it will normally take several years to build up significant cash value.**

4. **Legacy planning.** For example fund grandkids' education or leave a bequest to church or charity.

The elder son of one of our clients, a young man just starting a family of his own and getting his career going, came in to see us on the advice of his dad. He had a vague idea he needed life insurance, but when we drew a 4-square diagram illustrating these advantages of permanent life insurance, we could see the light bulb come on.

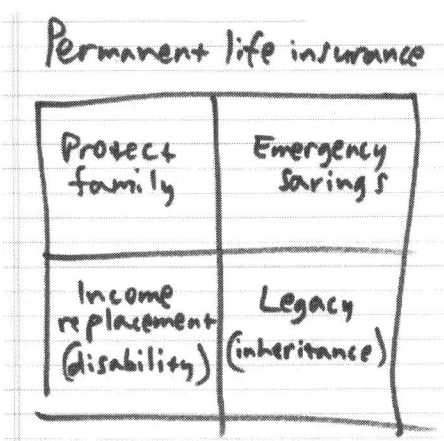

Life Insurance As An Enforced Savings Plan

It can be difficult for a younger family to find extra money in the household budget to build up bank savings. However life insurance premium payments tend to be treated as a necessity, a bill that absolutely must be paid…and meanwhile the life insurance cash value account steadily builds. So it's like an enforced savings plan and helpful in fulfilling critical financial planning goals in a unique way.

Buying lower-cost term life insurance and investing the difference could work similarly—however you should only buy term insurance if you definitely *don't* need the lasting protection of permanent insurance. And regardless of that…well, re-read the previous paragraph.

Taxation Of Life Insurance

- **Death benefit:** tax-free to beneficiary (except in the case of the "life insurance triangle of doom" explained below).

- **Cash value growth in whole life and universal life policies:** tax-free.

- **Dividends paid by the insurance company into whole life policies to build cash value, reduce premiums, or increase death benefit:** tax-free.

- **Withdrawals or loans from cash value:** tax-free up until you take out more than the total premiums you paid into the policy.

The Life Insurance Triangle Of Doom

Also known as the "Goodman Triangle" (after a 1946 court case) or "The Unholy Trinity": if the owner, insured, and beneficiary of a life insurance policy are *three different* persons or entities, the death benefit proceeds are *taxable* as a gift by the owner!

Example: husband owns the policy, wife is the insured, and the kids are the beneficiaries. Wife dies, policy pays $500,000 to the kids—and suddenly the husband owes gift tax.

Example: your company Widgets Inc. owns the policy, you (the business owner) are the insured, and your Widgets Inc. business partner Fran is the beneficiary. The plan in case of your death is for your business partner Fran to receive the life insurance proceeds and use it to buy the business from your widow—a common approach to business contingency planning. However in this example the business would be subject to gift tax.

To avoid this tax nightmare, simply make sure *two of the three participants in a life insurance policy are the same person or entity*. In the first example above, the wife could be both the owner and the insured, problem solved. In the second example, you (business owner) could be both the owner and insured (and the business could pay the premiums directly or indirectly in the form of a bonus to you). A buy/sell agreement would need to be drafted between you and your business partner Fran legally binding her to pay your widow the life insurance proceeds in order to own the business. Problem solved.

Questions You Must Ask Your Life Insurance Agent

1. **Are you independent, or captive?** An independent agent can shop the universe of companies for good terms for you. A captive agent is strictly limited to one insurance company.

2. **Am I over-insured, or under-insured?** This will change over time as your family, business, and financial circumstances change. Revisit this question on a regular basis.

3. **Is there a no-lapse guarantee included?** This ensures your policy will continue to a specified age regardless of interest rates and market performance in the broader economy. During the period following the 2008 recession when financial market interest rates were near zero for an extended period, insurance companies lost money on no-lapse policies they had issued previously; as a result of that experience, no-lapse policies issued since 2008 may not be as favorable as they once were. Guarantees may only go until age 90, or 95, with potentially much higher premiums for this feature.

4. **What growth rate assumption are you using on the cash value account, and how did you come up with that?** If it's unrealistically high, the policy may not perform as expected. This is of particular interest in Variable Universal Life and Indexed Universal Life policies, where cash value depends on stock market growth (unlike basic Universal Life where growth projections are based on current interest rates and/or guaranteed interest rates). For example instead of being able to skip premium payments with a Variable Universal Life policy, you may find yourself having to add extra payments because stock markets didn't perform as projected.

5. **What are the policy provisions for taking loans or withdrawals from cash value?** Even if you don't intend to use the cash value, you never know when that might change. Understand the rules and restrictions around accessing the money, including interest rates for loans against your policy's cash value, and how the policy might be affected if you choose

not to repay the loan (regardless, there would be no effect on your credit score—this is essentially a loan to yourself).

6. **Are there optional "living benefits" or "riders"?** Some policies allow you to access the death benefit value while you're still alive—for example in case of disability or terminal illness.

7. **In a "Participating Whole Life" policy, how will dividends be used?** Dividends may be used to purchase "paid up additions" (a larger death benefit), or to reduce premium payments, or simply to build up cash value.

8. **Should I replace my term policy now, or wait until the last minute?** Your agent should be able to "age you" by plugging in an earlier birth year, in order to estimate the cost of buying a new policy two or three years from now. (Caution: insurance rates may change, so these artificial projections should be taken with a grain of salt). In some cases it could make sense to lock in your current age and health by making the leap to a new policy sooner rather than later...but discuss the pros *and* cons with your insurance professional.

9. **Should I replace my term policy with permanent life insurance?** The older you get, the costlier this becomes...and some term policies don't allow conversion after a certain point, so check on this option 2-3 years before the term is up.

10. **Are my beneficiaries up to date?** If you've had a change in your family or business situation, make sure the insurance proceeds will go to the right person or entity.

11. **Is it time for a review?** If you have a Universal Life policy, the performance and longevity of your policy may depend on the interest rate environment or stock market cycles. Your agent should request an "in force illustration" periodically and review it with you. This ledger shows a projection of the cash value and face value (death benefit) of your policy into the future, so you can make sure it's properly funded to last as long as you need it to last.

A Life Insurance Strategy for "Lazy" Or "Crazy" Money

If you purchase a permanent life insurance policy with a single large sum of money up front, called a "single-pay premium," instead of paying regular premiums over time, it may become classified under IRS rules as a "modified endowment contract" (MEC).

Withdrawals of cash value from a MEC are taxed as ordinary income regardless of whether you're withdrawing more than the total premiums you paid, unlike a normal life insurance policy. However the death benefit is still tax-free to your heirs.

On one hand, if your intention is to withdraw or borrow cash value from the policy in the future, this may not be desirable when compared to a normal life insurance policy, where withdrawals are tax-free if you withdraw less than the total premiums you paid into the policy.

However if you have a large lump sum of money earning a low interest rate somewhere, for example $50,000 or $100,000 in a low-interest bank savings account—what we sometimes call "lazy money"—and it's earmarked to pass along to your heirs (in other words you *don't* intend to use the money yourself, and it's *not* part of your emergency fund), a MEC may make sense.

Our client Mr. D owned a Variable Universal Life policy which had been purchased for him by his employer several years prior as part of a "restricted executive bonus plan." Mr. D was a great employee, and this program was a type of "golden handcuffs" to potentially help retain him in the business: as long as he stayed with the company, they would pay the life insurance premiums, the policy would potentially build cash value over the years which Mr. D could use to supplement his retirement savings, and in the meantime his family would receive the protection of the death benefit.

After Mr. D retired he became the owner of the policy, which indeed had built up a decent amount of cash value. However Mr. D was a conservative investor, uncomfortable with "crazy" stock market fluctuations which affected that cash value negatively at times. He asked us if he could take all the cash out of the policy without affecting the life insurance benefit.

This wasn't feasible under the terms of that policy…so instead we transferred the cash value to a "MEC" policy, which preserved that existing cash value with no stock market exposure at all, gave his family some life insurance protection, and included a "return of premium" feature for the first five years in case he changed his mind and wanted the cash instead of the life insurance after all. If he kept the policy, after five years the cash account would start receiving a conservative interest rate of growth each year…and he could withdraw that full cash value any time (of course sacrificing the life insurance benefit in that case). This was an appealing option to Mr. D.

Unlike interest in a bank account, cash value in a MEC will grow tax deferred, similar to an annuity or IRA. And also as with an annuity, withdrawals of the growth beyond the total paid in will be taxed as ordinary income. But the amount of money the life insurance policy will pay to your heirs at your death could be significantly more than if you simply passed along a fixed-interest annuity, or low-interest bank savings…especially if you happen to die at a younger age than expected.

And to be clear, the death benefit of the life insurance is *tax-free* to your heirs, whether or not the policy was a MEC.

In other words you can leverage that "lazy money" into a potentially much larger and tax-free guaranteed inheritance for your heirs, thus maximizing this part of your legacy.

[Again, please note: distributions (withdrawals or policy loans) from life insurance policies treated as Modified Endowment Contracts ("MEC's") under Section 7702A of the Internal Revenue Code are subject to less favorable tax treatment than distributions from policies that are not

MEC's. If the policy is a MEC, distributions will be taxable to the extent there is any gain in the policy. In addition, if the policy owner is under age 59 ½ or is a corporation at the time of the distribution, there is a penalty tax of 10% on the taxable amount. Without regard to whether a policy is a MEC, a gain in the policy is taxable on full surrender of the policy. Please speak with your investment professional and/or tax professional about your individual situation.]

ᴦ ᴦ

RISK MANAGEMENT CRITICAL ZONE IV: DISABILITY INSURANCE

***BOTTOM LINE:** If it would be a financial problem to partially or entirely lose the employment income provided by someone in your household, look into disability insurance. Understand the most common policy provisions to find the right balance between cost and benefits.*

What is your most valuable financial asset? Your home? Your 401(k)? For most of us, the value of these tangible assets pale in comparison to the mountains of cash produced from a career's worth of work.

We like the analogy of a money tree growing in your back yard...producing a thousand dollars a week, or two thousand, or five thousand. If you had such a tree, would you insure it? Of course you would. The pay-earners in your home *are* like that money tree (but with personality!), and you should consider life insurance and disability income insurance to protect the ongoing harvest which keeps your household financially solvent.

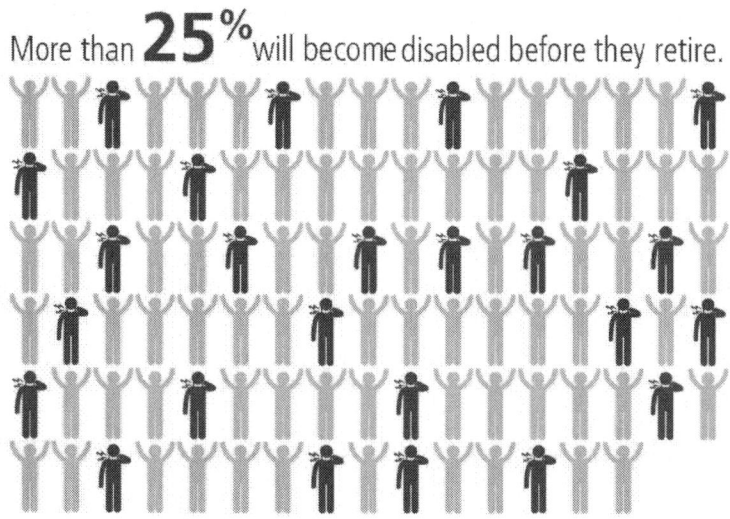
U.S. Social Security Administration, Fact Sheet, April 2, 2014

One in five adults in the U.S. lives with a disability (Centers For Disease Control 2015 report), and the average individual worker disability claim lasts over 31 months (U.S. Individual DI Risk Management Survey 2011). At any time during your working life, your odds of becoming disabled are much higher than your odds of dying.

If you were knocked out of work due to illness or injury, how long would your household budget hold up? As with all types of insurance, consider the worst-case scenario—no more income from your current age all the way through retirement.

If you qualify for Social Security disability you'll receive your full retirement age benefit. Visit ssa.gov if you don't know how much this is. Still, for many of our clients this would come nowhere close to meeting their income need.

Some workplaces offer group Short Term Disability and/or Long-term Disability plans. In many cases these policies are relatively inexpensive and provide decent coverage—up to a limit, typically 2/3 of your pay. Ask HR about the limits of your workplace plan if you have one.

But whether or not your workplace offers such a benefit, you should at least discuss free-standing disability insurance with your advisor to understand your options for protecting your income.

The provisions of individual disability policies vary widely from state to state, and from occupation to occupation, but here are the common moving parts to consider:

The policy's definition of disability: "Own occupation" means if you can't do your current job, the policy pays benefits. "Modified own occupation" means if you can only partially do your job, the policy pays benefits. "Any occupation" is more restrictive, meaning you have to be unable to do any job to receive benefits (specifics of these definitions may vary from policy to policy). Obviously "own occupation" is more expensive than the "any occupation" limitation, so weigh the importance of this to your situation.

The benefit amount: the amount of income replaced. This is typically a percentage of your full pay, typically 60% or 70%. Again, the richer the benefit, the more you pay for the policy.

The elimination period: This is like a "time deductible" requiring you to share the burden with the insurance company... a specific amount of time you have to wait after becoming disabled before policy payouts begin. This may be 30, 60, 90, or 180 days, or some other timeframe—or no elimination period at all if you're willing to pay dearly. Think through the cost compared to the benefit of a shorter or longer elimination period. And as with money deductibles on other kinds of insurance, make sure you save enough emergency funds to cover your household expenses during the elimination period.

The benefit period: How long benefits are paid. Many policies pay benefits to age 65, but other options may be available.

Taxation of premiums and benefits: The rule of thumb here is that the IRS wants tax to be paid on either the money which is subsequently used to pay premiums, or the money which is paid out as policy benefits—by someone. If your employer pays your premiums, the employer can normally deduct those from their taxes (so no tax is paid on the money used for policy premiums); therefore, you may have to pay tax on the benefits. If you pay the premiums yourself with after-tax dollars (take-home pay), you probably won't have to pay tax on the benefits. If you pay premiums with pre-tax (untaxed) dollars out of your paycheck, you may have to pay tax on the benefits. The IRS wants one side or the other to result in taxes, but not both. Fair enough!

RISK MANAGEMENT CRITICAL ZONE V: PROPERTY AND CASUALTY INSURANCE

***BOTTOM LINE:** Imagine worst-case home, auto, and business disaster scenarios and the potential impact on your finances and life. Review your policies periodically to make sure they're still the right fit. Use an agent with access to multiple companies and who understands your personal and/or business circumstances. Understand each provision of your policy, and consider an "umbrella" policy for additional liability coverage if appropriate.*

Spend sufficient time and effort selecting your property and casualty policy. When buying a home or business, there is such a flurry of decisions and expenses that it's easy just to purchase the minimum coverage required by the lender and move on. But this is not a decision you should rush, or try to just get by on the cheap. Renters: protecting your belongings from fire, theft, or damage may be quite inexpensive, as you're only insuring your possessions, not the building.

The most important link in this chain is your property and casualty insurance agent…start with a trusted agent through a referral from family, friends, or another advisor, or based on your own experience—and check the background of the agent and their company.

Use an agent who has access to multiple insurance companies in order to receive a competitive quote.

If you're a business owner, consider using an agent who works with others within your field and understands the special circumstances and potential liabilities you face. An agent who specializes in coverage for public event venues may not do the best job if your business is a turkey farm (even though there may be some overlap there in more ways than one!).

This may be especially true if you use multiple agents. Working with one trusted agent may be the best approach, as they'll typically have a good understanding of which companies have favorable underwriting processes and customer service, and may also have knowledge of which companies are easiest to work with when you have a claim.

Take time to understand the coverage limits of your policies, and take the trouble to engage your agent to *imagine worst case scenarios*...the agent should be able to paint a realistic picture of a situation that would result in more liability than a particular policy would cover. How many people would have to be injured on your property, and how badly, before you would exceed the coverage limits of your policy? You need to understand what kind of situations would push the limits of your insurance policies.

In a worst-case scenario where you lost a lawsuit, how would you pay the judgment against you…garnished wages? Existing savings? Liens on property or other assets? What is it worth to you on a monthly or annual basis to transfer that risk to an insurance company?

Once you have a few worst case scenarios in mind, you should also consider how you can best *prevent* such scenarios through home maintenance and repair, adding safety features, monitoring activity on your property or business, and so on.

Be sure special items such as guns, musical instruments, jewelry, collectibles etc. are covered—via riders on your policy if necessary—and keep the list of items updated with the insurance company.

For your home, ask if mold coverage is available…and will it be covered if it's the result of water damage from fighting a fire?

Should you combine your auto policy with your homeowner policy to save money? That's fine if both policies meet your needs. Such an arrangement may be especially efficient if it also qualifies you for **"umbrella" coverage** (higher liability limits—see below).

Asking questions like these will show your agent you're serious about getting this right.

Umbrella liability coverage: This can increase your liability coverage up to $1,000,000 or $2,000,000 or more. In some cases it may be much less expensive than you expect, especially if you combine your auto and homeowner policy with the same company, and already have a liability limit higher than the bare minimum. It may be a very inexpensive leap to get umbrella coverage and really account for those worst-case scenarios you and your agent came up with.

And as with all types of insurance, don't neglect to review your policy every few years to make sure it's still what you need.

RISK MANAGEMENT CRITICAL ZONE VI: LONG-TERM CARE INSURANCE (AND AN ALTERNATIVE)

BOTTOM LINE: Understand the asset protection features of

long-term care insurance in your State, as well as the potential health- and lifestyle-protection benefits. Imagine helping your spouse (or your spouse helping you) with the activities of daily living all day every day—including the heavy lifting that may be required to help a partner get in and out of bed, chairs, baths, etc., and the potentially disastrous strain on the health of the caregiver.

Learn about the costs of long-term care in your area, and the types of facilities and services that are covered.

Medicaid can help with long-term care, but not until you "spend-down" your assets in order to qualify for public assistance. Long-term care insurance may help solve this problem.

A single-premium "life plus long-term care" insurance policy may help eliminate the two main objections to insurance: potentially rising premiums, and permanent loss of the money spent on premiums whether you use the insurance or not.

Understand the "moving parts" of any long-term care insurance product you're considering by getting professional guidance when shopping for a policy.

A 2012 MetLife Mature Market Institute study found the average cost of nursing home care in the U.S. was over $81,000 per year, and in-home health care average cost is about $21 per hour—and inflation keeps driving the costs up.

So who is the caregiver in your family when someone is sick?

How about when that someone's health starts really failing…when they can't get up out of their chair on their own, or go to the bathroom by themselves, or bathe, or feed themselves?

How many times per day do you need to get out of your chair?

What if someone had to help you every single time?

If you're a couple, who is going to help you each time? What about when you're 80-90 years old, how much harder will it be to help your spouse—or for your spouse to help you—out of that chair that many times? If you're the primary caregiver in your home, how is that going to affect your own health?

And when all that starts wearing you down physically, and your own health and strength start to suffer…and you're still the primary caregiver, then you may face the biggest question of your life: *who cares for the caregiver?*

This is a real problem for many couples whose long-term care plan was the "sweetheart plan": I'll take care of you, you take care of me.

The kids can help, but a big concern for many of our clients is that someday they'll be a burden to their adult children. They are happy to assist, but they have lives, jobs, their own children to care for…and again, how many times per day will you need help getting out of that chair?

The odds are in favor of this being a real problem in your life. According to the 2010 Prudential Long-term Care Cost Study, a 65-year-old has a 70% chance of needing long-term care at some point. For those age 85 and over, 51.5% were living in a nursing home prior to death (2015, Employee Benefit Research Institute, "Utilization Patterns And Out-Of-Pocket Expenses for Different Health Care Services Among American Retirees.")

When you think about how long you might live, do you pick a number *lower* than 85? If not, are you willing to gamble on the odds of a coin flip whether you should prepare for the possibility of needing long-term care?

In our retirement planning presentations for the public, we talk about the average cost per year in our own city for assisted living, and for nursing home care. Research costs in your own area, and whether the inflation rate for these services is higher than the "normal" inflation rate. Many people discover that prices are high enough to potentially derail their retirement plans, including plans to leave assets to heirs.

We ask almost every prospective client if they have long-term care insurance...not because everyone should have it, but because everyone should at least know it exists, how it works, what it costs, and what it may cost *not* to have it. Nearly everyone we meet who has watched a loved one deal with long-term care is very interested in this topic, and eager to learn what they can do to prepare.

As we mentioned elsewhere (and this bears repeating): Mr. and Mrs. R came in to see us after one of our events and this was certainly on their minds. They had done a great job saving money during their working years, and recently Mrs. R had inherited some money from her father—so they were able to enjoy a comfortable retirement. But when we asked about their long-term care planning, she said, "We asked our current investment advisor the same thing. She held up our quarterly investment statement and said, "Well...this *is* your long-term care plan!'"

Self-insuring is a possibility if you have millions of dollars and don't mind potentially burning through a good part of it.

What about Medicare? Medicare covers medical expenses including a short period in a skilled nursing facility following a hospital stay, but it does not cover long-term "custodial" care (long-term nursing home residency, assisted living, in-home assistance, etc.).

Medicaid will help, but there's a huge catch: the spend-down rule. Medicaid is for people who have limited resources and nowhere else to turn. As of this writing, a couple is required to spend their assets down to $2,000 before Medicaid will step in (ask your advisor about current rules). That means potentially a lifetime of savings wiped out by just a few years of expensive custodial care.

Medicaid may let you keep your house (but may put a lien on it in order to recover long-term care costs from your heirs after you're gone)—otherwise your savings account, your IRA, your cash, even the cash value of a permanent life insurance policy, and most of your income from whatever sources you have, may go toward your custodial care.

So we're faced with two enormous challenges:

1. **Getting help** with what professional caregivers refer to as "activities of daily living" or ADL's: getting up and down from your chair and getting from place to place in the home (commonly called "transferring"); dressing; feeding oneself; and personal hygiene including bathing, grooming, and using the restroom. Age and poor health may gradually turn these activities into an overwhelming burden for the primary caregiver in your home. And the longer that primary caregiver waits to get help, the worse the situation can become for both.

2. **The Medicaid spend-down rule** if and when it's time to get professional assistance in the home or in an assisted living facility or nursing home…you can't get Medicaid assistance with the expenses until you've used up almost all of your own savings.

Most people assume long-term care insurance only addresses the expense of getting help with those ADL's. And the value of that should not be underestimated—because you may be more likely to get the skilled help you need *in your home* sooner if you have insurance to cover some or all of the costs. And if you get help sooner, you just might be able to stay healthier longer, enjoy a better quality of life, and *stay in your home longer.* How much is that worth?

As for the Medicaid spend-down problem: the majority of people we meet don't realize that long-term care insurance can also potentially address this critical issue. Long-term care policies are typically structured so that your monthly premiums are essentially buying a pool of money to be used for long-term care expenses. And in most states, Medicaid sees that pool of money as self-insurance—so **Medicaid may allow you keep an equivalent amount of your own savings, protected from the spend-down rule. (IMPORTANT:** your State may require specific policy provisions in order to qualify for Medicaid spend-down protection. For example a policy may be required to include inflation protection—annually increasing the long term care monthly benefit provided by the policy. Also keep in mind that Medicaid is for low-income individuals, so if your retirement income is too high you may not qualify for Medicaid anyway.)

Because of this potential protection from Medicaid spend-down rules, you may be able to continue using your retirement savings for the other things you always planned: funding and sharing "the good life" with family and friends, building a legacy, and perhaps passing it on to heirs.

So long-term care insurance doesn't just address the risk that someday one of you may need help getting up out of that chair all day every day. It also addresses the risk that you'll have to spend down your hard earned savings. All the way down to $2,000.

According to a 2014 study by Boston College Center For Retirement Research, if you have very little savings to begin with, the spend-down rule may not be a big deal. But if you've worked your whole life to save $100,000, or $500,000, or a few million dollars, and you have the potential to spend a few years in a nursing home, blowing through tens of thousands of dollars per year...what would it be worth to simply transfer that expense to an insurance company?

The ultimate cost of your long-term care is a big unknown...buying long-term care insurance trades that "unknown" for a "known," which can help you manage toward your other retirement goals.

What Types Of Long-term Care Facilities Are Covered?

Comprehensive policies typically cover you in the following places **(make sure you understand what is covered in any specific policy you're considering)**:

- Your home
- Adult day care facility
- Assisted living / residential care / alternate care facility
- Nursing home
- Alzheimer's special care facility
- Hospice care facility

And provide assistance with the following needs:

- Getting around
- Personal care (eating, bathing, dressing, grooming, etc.)
- Hospice (end of life) care
- Respite care (providing breaks for caregivers, for example if you have a family member as a primary caregiver, a respite care provider may come to your home one or two days per week to give the primary caregiver a much-needed break).

Policies typically have a "waiting period" before coverage kicks in, during which time you have to fund the expenses yourself. The longer the waiting period, the less expensive the insurance...it's a form of cost-sharing much like a deductible on health insurance or car insurance. Choosing a very short or "zero" waiting period may be more expensive than it's worth—as is also often the case when you choose a low deductible with other kinds of insurance—so put pencil to paper and try out various scenarios for your circumstances to determine whether paying more for a shorter waiting period is worth it, and where your break-even point lies: how much extra will you pay per year for the short waiting period? How many years until the total of that extra expense would have covered the expenses you might expect to face during a longer waiting period? Then make sure you have sufficient emergency savings to fill the waiting period coverage gap.

A Long-term Care Insurance Alternative

There is another option for long-term care funding that may eliminate the two most common complaints against traditional long-term care insurance (and insurance in general): "Premiums can go up" and, "If we don't use it, we wasted our money on the premiums and can't get it back."

There are a few life insurance companies that offer a special kind of life insurance policy with a long-term care feature (rider), along with the option of a "single-pay" premium (fully funded with an up-front lump sum)—and also a "return of premium" feature that allows you to get back some or all of what you paid in.

These policies have the added benefit of the life insurance component, which may pass money to heirs in the form of a tax-free death benefit (however use of the long-term care benefits may count against the life insurance death benefit).

The way it typically works is this:

- As with regular life insurance, you complete an application including authorization for the insurance company to review your medical records and complete a physical exam and/or health interview.
- If you receive an offer of insurance, you may pay a lump sum up front with some policies (instead of ongoing premiums).

The amount you pay will determine how much life insurance and long-term care coverage you receive.

- There are no further premiums after the single lump sum payment. This eliminates the possibility of a future premium increase as is the case with traditional long-term care insurance.

- Your one-time premium payment purchases two benefits:

    1. The life insurance benefit which passes to your named beneficiary at your death. It's important to understand that this special type of policy typically won't provide as large a death benefit as "normal" single-premium life insurance would provide, due to the simultaneous funding of long-term care benefits. However depending on your lifespan, the modest death benefit provided by a life-plus-long-term-care policy may still be an excellent return on your investment. Another important consideration is that the death benefit will be reduced if you exercise the long-term care features, often on a dollar-for-dollar basis...in other words, the more you use the long-term care features, the less life insurance death benefit will remain.

    2. The long-term care component which, like traditional long-term care insurance, provides a pool of money to be used for specific expenses—most or all of the same expenses covered by traditional long-term care insurance. The size of this pool of funds depends on how large an initial premium you paid, along with the insurance company's underwriting decision based your health, age, and other factors. The younger and healthier you are when you purchase the policy, the larger the pool of coverage your lump sum will purchase.

- The "return of premium" feature available on some policies typically provides a partial return of premium for a period of time, then full return of premium after that specified period.

Policies vary, so work with your advisor to shop the current marketplace.

A return-of-premium policy means your decision to give up a large sum of money doesn't have to be final...if you decide you need the money for something else, or simply don't want to continue the policy, you can walk away whole. However it's important to understand that the refund will not include any interest or growth for the period of time that the insurance company had the money...it's as if you made an interest-free loan to the insurance company.

- **Important:** The guarantees of any insurance policy are only as good as the company making the promises. Make sure you work with an experienced, qualified agent to seek a highly rated company with a good track record.

Ironically, getting either traditional long-term care insurance or the single-premium "life plus long-term care" with return of premium feature may be difficult if you're not in decent health; and it's harder to get the older you get.

It pays to think ahead, and understand your options by speaking with a qualified professional—and if it makes sense for your situation, "lock in" your age and health with the purchase of insurance while you're still able.

RISK MANAGEMENT CRITICAL ZONE VII: IDENTITY THEFT AND SCAM PROTECTION

***BOTTOM LINE:** Guard your personal information as if your financial life depends on it—because it may.*

Buy a shredder, and use it.

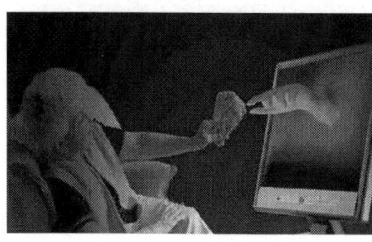

Don't click on email links from unknown senders; and don't give your Social Security number, bank or investment account numbers, or personally identifiable information (dates of birth, address, etc.) over the phone or elsewhere, unless you really know who you're talking to...in other words don't let someone trick you into giving up personal information.

Check your credit report every year (or up to three times per year—for free).

Protect your wallet and your smartphone (and other digital devices), and protect your credit and debit cards from "skimmer" devices at ATM's or elsewhere.

Don't broadcast on social media that you're on vacation, as this is an open invitation to burglars who may break into your home and steal more than just your identity.

Review the "Real Estate Income Considerations" section of the Investing chapter for tips on avoiding scams by rental tenants.

As the information age has progressed to the point where you can carry a computer in your pocket, so has the danger of having your identity stolen. Take some basic precautions to protect yourself:

Trash and trusters: The vast majority of identity theft happens two ways: "social engineering" and "trash mining" (literally digging through your trash containers—so *always* shred documents that contain account information or personally identifiable information like Social Security numbers and dates of birth).

"Social engineering" involves tricking someone to give up

information that can be used to steal your identity or your money. For example an email that looks legitimate and which contains a link to what looks like an official website, where you enter your user name and password…and suddenly you've been had. Look at the website address every single time before entering sensitive data to make sure it's not slightly off (myXYZbank.com instead of XYZbank.com for example).

Another type of social engineering comes in the form of a letter, phone call, or even a knock at the door from someone claiming to be from the IRS, FEMA, or some other official-sounding agency. For example someone "from the IRS" may call and threaten to sue or take possession of your assets due to a tax debt…this often works when they reach someone who actually *does* owe taxes! But the IRS will never call you about a debt, they will send a letter (but of course scammers send "IRS" letters too).

Ultimately a scammer will ask for personally identifiable information, account information, or even ask directly for money, including requests for disposable debit cards, wires, or money orders.

Mailbox theft, especially during tax season, is another favorite of identity thieves. Try not to leave checks, Social Security numbers, or account numbers out there with the red flag up…that is an open invitation. Instead, use a public mail collection box, or better yet, go online and set up automatic bank drafts for your recurring bills and payments. But use precautions there as well—look for a padlock symbol in the internet address box to help verify that a website is secure.

As of this writing, bank ATM's are still vulnerable to a device scammers attach right over the card reader; this device saves information from your card when you slide it (or transmits it wirelessly to the nearby thief), and/or hides a small camera which captures you entering your PIN. Later the thief retrieves the device, and they now have the data of every customer who used that ATM. The bank doesn't even know it happened unless they catch the thief in the act. Look closely at the card reader when you use an ATM…and give it a little tug before sliding your card. If something seems amiss, notify the bank.

Protect your wallet when in public by keeping it in your front pocket or a zipped pocket of your purse; password-protect your smartphone. Be careful with Wi-Fi networks in hotels: don't assume the network you link to with your smartphone or tablet doesn't belong to a criminal. Ask the front desk for the name of their network first.

Wait until you're back at home to gush about your wonderful vacation. Criminals troll social media sites looking for opportunities to break into homes without having to worry about someone walking in on them. And have your mail held or forwarded while you're gone, or picked up daily (and in a timely manner) by someone you trust.

Finally, check your credit report at least once per year, or up to three times per year if you suspect trouble. There are three major credit reporting agencies (Experian, Equifax, and Trans Union), and you can go directly to each of their websites for a free report once per year. This means you could put them on a rotation and review a fresh free report every four months. Look for unusual or unexpected activity, accounts you don't recognize, a home address that's not yours—anything out of the ordinary.

If your identity is stolen, notify the authorities and all companies with whom you have accounts, and get ready for a whole lot of trouble. Better to prevent this nightmare than to ever have to deal with the consequences!

Risk Management For Business Owners

In addition to "all of the above," you must take critical extra steps to protect your company and the income it produces for your family. Your special risk management considerations generally fall into these categories:

- Death of owner: if your spouse is designated to inherit the business, but has no intention of actually taking over, what will happen? If they have to find a buyer, who manages operations in the meantime? You need to establish buy-sell provisions *now*.

    - Identify who will take over: partner(s), family, employee(s), or third-party purchaser? If it's a family member or employee, initiate in-depth discussions about how this would actually work, all the way through a successful transition for the business, employees, and customers.

    - Prepare a written buy-sell agreement with the assistance of an experienced attorney. This lays out a purchase price formula (which should be revisited regularly to make sure it remains suitable as conditions change), the responsibilities of each party, and other provisions.

    - Determine how the buy-sell agreement will be funded. Life insurance is a common method, with the current owner as the insured, and successor-owner as beneficiary and owner of the policy. This can provide immediate cash for the successor-owner to purchase the business from the surviving spouse. There are many variations on this theme, so work with an experienced business planner.

    - If the new owner will be an employee or family member, start to prepare them *now* to successfully take over and keep the business alive and thriving. Incidentally this may uncover ways to make your business better in general, while you're still kicking!

    - Consider "stay-put" agreements to commit key managers and employees to assisting with the transition to new ownership in case of your death, with a "stay bonus" (in addition to regular pay) as an incentive to stick around.

- Disability/illness/injury of owner: In addition to income replacement insurance for yourself, consider business overhead expense insurance as well if you're the "haymaker"—if you're not bringing in the revenue due to disability, the bills still get paid and the doors stay open.

- Death or disability of key employee: how long would it take to find a replacement for your top manager or salesperson? How much revenue would the business potentially lose during that transition? Consider key-person life insurance and disability insurance to prepare for this contingency.

- Resignation of key employee: consider an Executive Bonus Plan to "golden handcuff" your key employee(s). A common method is to contribute to a cash-value life insurance policy on behalf of the employee. The life insurance component provides family protection, and the cash value can supplement their retirement savings someday. This shows the employee how much they mean to you in a concrete way; vesting provisions in an accompanying written agreement put teeth in the program—if they leave before the vesting period is complete, they sacrifice some or all of the benefit.

- Commercial property and casualty insurance, which may also include "business continuation" provisions to cover business expenses and payroll during down-time following a disaster.

- Industry-specific liability insurance: malpractice insurance and "errors and omissions" policies are necessities in certain fields.

You may need a number of risk-management specialists to help address these potential hazards to your livelihood and sweat-equity. Work with experienced professionals to weigh costs and benefits; you may wish to engage with a business advisor separately from your personal financial advisor if they're not experienced in these matters.

4.

Investing

I don't want to recommend investments we wouldn't use for our own money. I want to be able to look clients in the eye and tell them that.

-John Piatchek

BOTTOM LINE: Be an informed consumer; take the time to develop a basic understanding of investing concepts and products. Ask questions of your investment advisor—you don't have to be an expert, but if you don't understand an investment well enough to describe it to someone else reasonably well, don't proceed. There are always alternatives.

Nobody has ever consistently beaten the stock market over the long run. Fortunately you don't need to beat the market to take advantage of the significant growth potential it may provide for your portfolio.

Before pulling out of the stock markets in favor of "safety," make sure you really understand the various types of stock market risk and how you may be able to manage some of those risks—and whether some market exposure might still make sense for longer-term planning goals (and as a means to try to keep ahead of inflation).

If you still want out, there are many alternatives in addition to (but also including) bank products.

Evaluate your risk tolerance in terms of both your emotional reaction to market volatility and your investment time horizon. Understand our Recession Reserve™ approach to asset allocation which can help you find the right balance for you.

Understand how the sequence of market returns can affect your outcome if you're taking regular withdrawals from market investments.

Gain a basic understanding of income-producing investments, including rental real estate and others.

Learn about the tax ramifications (both positive and negative) of investment vehicles and investment decisions.

Be a disciplined investor.

Don't put too many eggs in one basket (diversify!).

Always keep one eye on expenses (including fund turnover), as cost is a primary factor in investment success: the less you give someone else, the more there is for your portfolio to build upon.

If you manage some or all of your own investments: study hard, study often, and get a second opinion from an experienced professional (or more than one) on a regular basis.

Business owners: diversify (don't let your company be the only "big egg" in your investment basket); if feasible, install a workplace retirement plan with your own goals in mind; select a cost-efficient plan (in terms of plan fees and investment choices).

NOTE: All investments involve varying levels and types of risks. These risks can be associated with the specific investment, or with the marketplace as a whole. Loss of principal is possible.

Using asset allocation or diversification as part of your investment strategy neither assures nor guarantees better performance and cannot protect against loss of principal due to changing market conditions.

THE TEAM

Almost everyone needs sooner or later:
  Financial planning professional
  Investment professional (some CFP®, ChFC or other financial
    planning professionals are qualified for this role).

And for some:
  Real estate agent or broker

DO-SOME-OF-IT-YOURSELFERS: We believe do-it-yourself investors are notoriously bad at it. This has been shown in study after study. In fact amateur investors can make such consistently poor decisions that there's a professional investing strategy which simply attempts to do exactly the opposite of amateur investors. "Cabinet" stocks are the industry term for partial lots (less than 100 shares) of a stock. If the supply of cabinet stocks goes up, it means amateurs are buying. This is considered a selling signal for professionals who seek to benefit from their belief that "amateur investors are always wrong." If the supply of cabinet stocks goes down, this means amateurs are selling, which these professionals see as a buying signal. This technique has been shown to be effective in some studies. On the other hand, we don't recommend you try this at home, as other factors may come into play...and amateurs just can't *always* be wrong!

Having said all that...some of our clients enjoy managing their own online brokerage accounts for a portion of their assets, and have varying degrees of success.

Some people go so far as to develop some real investing expertise, and may do a fine job of managing all of their own investments. If you believe you're one of those people, we encourage you to occasionally get a second opinion anyway. It's been said that an attorney who represents himself has a fool for a client, and a doctor should never try to treat themselves. Why do "they" say that? Because it's sometimes difficult to look at your own situation objectively...hard to see the forest when you're busy tending to individual trees. Especially when it's your forest, your trees.

We share additional thoughts in the "Do-It-Yourself-Investor Dangers" section at the end of this chapter.

How it works in the real world: Our client Mr. J had recently retired, and relocated from Illinois to Missouri. Several years prior he had invested significant sums of money in a couple of "note programs"—illiquid investments which were meant to distribute income to Mr. J for a few years, and then return his principal to him.

He also held three other market investment accounts with an advisor in his former state of residence, using stock and bond mutual funds in a traditional IRA, a Roth IRA, and a "non-qualified" (non-IRA) account.

To keep the IRA tax deferral working in his favor, we earmarked the non-IRA account for his short- to mid-term income needs to supplement Social Security. We placed those funds in a liquid (easily available) conservative bond index fund allocation which offered stability but with better growth potential than bank savings. By using index funds we lowered Mr. J's investment expenses, thereby potentially improving performance. We used primarily short- and mid-term bond funds because we were in a very low interest rate environment at the time—when bond interest starts rising, bond values drop, but using short- and mid-term bonds can help reduce this negative effect if interest rates begin to go up.

We knew Mr. J would have to start taking IRS-required distributions from the traditional IRA starting at age 70 ½ in a few years. Those payouts would be plenty enough to meet his income needs, so our strategy would be to shift the non-IRA account to a more aggressive allocation at that time...because Mr. J has a high risk tolerance, and a more aggressive allocation has better long-term growth potential.

We earmarked the Roth IRA as an inheritance for Mr. J's son. As a non-spouse beneficiary, the son would have to take IRS-required distributions on the inherited account, but those distributions would be stretched over the son's life expectancy...and free of Federal and State tax (as would be any ongoing growth in the remaining account). Again we invested aggressively using low-cost index funds. This account would see a lot of volatility (ups and downs) over shorter periods, but over the long run would take advantage of the capital markets' growth potential.

As for those two old note programs: Mr. J continued to receive some income from one of them; the other one stopped paying distributions entirely, and finally returned a small fraction of his original principal to him at an overall significant loss which he would never be able to recover.

Fortunately Mr. J had plenty of other resources to meet his needs, so the losses he suffered in those failed investments, although painful, did not derail his long-term goals.

We don't believe Mr. J's former advisor intentionally did anything wrong, and neither does Mr. J…those note programs were with companies which had performed well in the past, but economic conditions simply took an unexpected wrong turn against those particular holdings. We explained that we occasionally use similar types of income-focused products for our clients, but that we and our broker-dealer exercise intensive due diligence because of the inherent risks. The offerings Mr. J purchased in Illinois were never on our "approved" list for our clients.

This illustrates the importance of doing your own due diligence on your advisor and on any products you are offered…and it's always more than okay to get a second opinion if you are offered something out of the ordinary.

Tired Of The Stock Market Roller Coaster?

Before you get out of the markets, ask yourself these questions:

- Am I following my gut, or am I following the math? (See our discussion of this concept below.)

- What's my time horizon for long-term accumulation goals? Short-term spending and/or emergency funds?

- Am I avoiding investment options that might be a good fit for some of my goals?

In the end if you can't sleep at night because of your stock market exposure, do something about it: fix the issues in your portfolio which may be increasing your risk, implement a strategy to reduce the potential effect of temporary market dips, or get out of the markets. Just make sure you've explored your options first, because the stock markets are historically (in our opinion) an excellent hedge against another kind of risk: the risk that you won't get enough growth in your investments to keep up with inflation.

Investment Risk And Your Risk Tolerance

If all you picture when you hear the words "investment risk" is that you're in danger of losing your money, you may retreat in irrational fear. If you overestimate—or underestimate—the real risks that exist, you may put your financial plan in hazard.

"Risk tolerance" is about your timeline, your goals, and to some degree your emotional reaction to investment volatility and other risk factors that come with investments.

When investment professionals talk about risk, in most cases they're not referring to the risk of total loss which might exist with speculative investments. "Speculative" investments are those which may have little or no track record, or may not be well diversified, or may have additional types of risk to a degree that makes them unsuitable for many investors. An example would be an inventor raising money to develop and market a new product; if you hand $10,000 to them, the risk of true loss may be significant. (See the "Speculative Investments" section later in this chapter.)

The broader well-regulated investment markets (bank savings

accounts and CD's, individual stocks on the major exchanges, mutual funds, exchange traded funds, REIT's, annuities, etc.) may be less speculative—especially if your portfolio is diversified—but there are still certain risks.

Systematic Investment Risk: Can't Stop This!

The following investment risks are known as "systematic" because they're built into the stock and bond markets, and diversifying your portfolio (spreading your money across many individual stocks, bonds, or commodities) *won't* help you avoid them.

- **"Market" risk.** Stock, bond, and commodities markets naturally vary over time with the ups and downs of the general economic environment.

- **"Purchasing power" (inflation) risk.** Prices for goods and services rise over time. Your investment growth potential must be greater than the inflation rate or you're going backward.

Purchasing Power of the US Dollar 1913-2013

Bureau of Labor Statistics. Calculation based on consumer price index; August 1913 = 100%. Data as of August 2013.

- **Interest rate risk.** When inflation rises, interest rates may rise as well. Higher interest rates may be great for bank savings and CD's, but terrible for home mortgage rates…and potentially bad for stock and bond values.

- **Reinvestment rate risk.** This is related to interest rate risk. An example is when an investor's bonds mature and it's time to reinvest the money into new bonds, and new bonds pay a lower interest rate, resulting in a monetary loss.

- **Exchange rate risk.** The value of the U.S. dollar in the world market is relative to other countries' currency values. If you own a foreign bond and the value of the U.S. dollar gets stronger compared to the value of the currency in the other country, the interest payments will be converted to fewer dollars. This risk may also affect stocks because it may reduce companies' profits when they export their goods; on the other hand a strong dollar is good for companies that import manufacturing supplies, as each dollar buys relatively more from a country with weaker currency.

Unsystematic Risk: Diversify, Diversify, Diversify!

The following "unsystematic" risks are the ones that a diversified portfolio (spread across many stock and bonds) may help reduce.

- **Business risk.** This is the ever-present risk that a company will perform poorly, causing their stock value to drop (or their bonds to default). Worst case, a company goes bankrupt and their stock and/or bond values may go to zero. Broad diversification helps reduce this hazard.

- **Accounting risk.** This is the risk that a company is "cooking the books." Owning a diversified portfolio can help spread out the impact, because presumably most companies don't engage in such shenanigans.

- **Financial risk / "default risk."** This is the risk of company default which may increase when a company takes on too much debt.

- **Liquidity and marketability risk.** This is about how quickly and easily an investment can be converted to cash, or sold on the free market. Very small company stocks may be more subject to this risk. This is not typically a problem for broadly diversified mutual fund or ETF portfolios.

- **Political risk, also known as "country risk" or "sovereign risk."** This is the risk that a company may have trouble profiting in a particular country due to political turmoil. Spreading your international holdings across several countries helps reduce this risk.

- **Executive risk.** This is the risk that bad management may cause a company to perform poorly or fail.

- **Government/regulation/tax risk.** Government regulations, taxes, and tariffs may hurt a company's ability to make a profit…and therefore potentially hurt stock performance. Having your assets spread across many countries can help reduce this risk, as with all "unsystematic" risk.

Diversifiable Risk	Non-Diversifiable Risk
Business	Market Risk
Accounting	Inflation
Financial	Interest Rates
Liquidity	Reinvestment Risk
Political	Exchange Rates
Executive	
Government	

Risk Tolerance: "Gut-Check" Or Math Problem?

The word "risk" can sound scary when you're talking about investments, especially your precious retirement savings. It may create an image of your money being in danger of a total loss, like at a casino.

Again, if your retirement savings is "non-diversified," for example you put it all in one company stock, well that actually is the kind of risk you'd be taking.

But if you spread your savings across a *minimum* of thirty or forty stocks using various styles and sectors, or in mutual funds or index funds holding dozens, hundreds, or thousands of stocks, you're considered to be "diversified."

When you're diversified, the word "risk" simply means "volatility," or the normal ups and downs of the broad stock market. Those ups and downs generally range from small daily swings of 0.1 - 0.5% either direction, to the 3-5% drops that may happen a couple of times most years, to 10% "corrections" which may happen every 1.5 - 2 years…to recessions that may occur every five to ten years or so, where the markets drop 10% - 40% or more.

Unfortunately you never know when these dips are going to happen, but you can be sure they will.

But if you plan for those inevitable swings, you can potentially reduce the chances of suffering a true loss which can happen if you sell during a downturn. This is the goal with our Recession Reserve™ approach to portfolio allocation.

What's Your Recession Reserve™?

Investors are reminded during most years that the stock market can be a roller coaster. So let's look at your investment "risk tolerance" in a different way, potentially drive some of the jitters out of investing, and maybe allow you to seek more growth potential.

"Risk tolerance" as typically measured by investment advisors is the degree to which you are willing or able to accept fluctuations in the value of your investments. If your risk tolerance is low, you want conservative, stable investments. High risk tolerance means you're fine with bigger short-term swings in exchange for more long-term growth potential.

Although the word "risk" itself implies danger of true loss, the U.S. stock market has been positive for 74% of years from 1927-2016, and all 15-year periods have been positive during that time ("Reasonable Return Expectations," DST Systems, Inc., 2016). Sharing in potential market growth is as easy as owning a broadly diversified basket of stocks, as long as you see it as a long-term proposition.

But there are two ways you can actually lose money in the stock market:

1. Own stock in a single company which defaults; the stock value may drop to zero. That's true loss. But it's easy to avoid disaster—don't hold more than 5% (preferably much less) of your investments in any single company stock. Winners offset losers in a diversified portfolio, so owning a broad pooled fund investment may do the trick by including dozens or thousands of stocks.

2. Sell securities for less than you paid…for example buy a broad U.S. index fund when markets are doing well, then sell during a recession for a lower price per share. Again, true loss.

So why do people "sell low"? Sometimes it's an emotional reaction to a market drop—"I'm losing money, so I'm getting out now." Understandable, but again, true loss.

The cure is to recognize that markets always perform in cycles, and a lower account balance is not really a loss *unless you sell*. Hang on, weather the downturn, and don't sell low out of an emotional overreaction.

But here's the other reason people sell their investments low and lose real money: they simply need to raise cash. Retirees often fall into this camp—regularly liquidating part of their portfolio to pay the bills and have their fun. That was the plan, right?

But this version of selling low can also be avoided, with a simple math exercise to create your Recession Reserve™:

First, market downturns are unpredictable, so assume the next recession starts tomorrow.

Next, understand that recessions tend to last about six months to a year-and-a-half; afterward, stock values start climbing back up, sometimes slowly, sometimes dramatically, in fits and starts. Through twenty-eight market downturns from the Great Depression through the 2008 recession, it took an average of 3.3 years for the purchasing value of stocks to return to full value (adjusting for inflation, and reinvesting stock dividends); the 2008 recession took about 5.3 years to play out, and in only four of those twenty-eight downturns did it take more than six years for stock values to recover ("Don't Fear The Bear," Mark Hulbert, Wall Street Journal, 2014).

So assume a five-year dip for a recession starting tomorrow, until stocks return to full value.

Now, how much cash will you need from your investments over the next five years? (Or seven years if you want to be extra-cautious?) Stop right now and figure that out. Got it?

Okay, that's how much you should consider taking out of the stock market right now, and putting into a more stable holding. This is your "Recession Reserve™."

What should you use for your "non-stock" Recession Reserve™ allocation? Anything with relatively stable value and sufficient liquidity can serve this function: a short- to intermediate-term bond fund, CD's, cash (if bank interest rates are attractive), or a fixed annuity or equity indexed annuity **(again taking care to account for any liquidity restrictions—remember this portion of your investments needs to be available for spending during market downturns)**.

When a market downturn comes along, simply draw needed cash from your Recession Reserve™ instead of selling stocks.

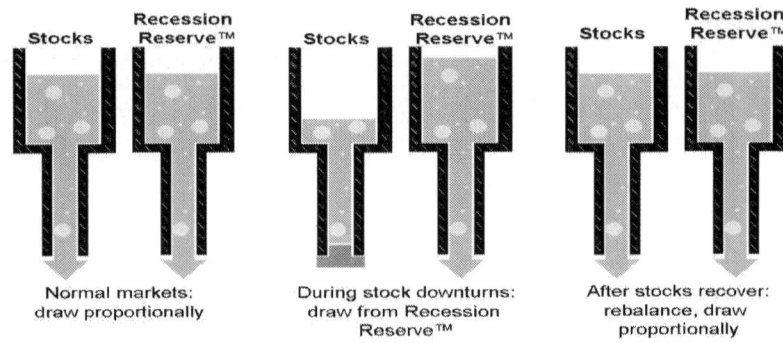

Normal markets: draw proportionally

During stock downturns: draw from Recession Reserve™

After stocks recover: rebalance, draw proportionally

If your "emotional" risk tolerance is very aggressive, this simple math approach can help you prevent being overweight to stocks and putting your financial plan in potential danger.

On the other hand, if you're a conservative investor who needs more growth to meet your goals, this may allow you to seek more market exposure with your long-term funds while remaining conservative with assets you'll need sooner.

We manage several workplace retirement plans in our city, and an employee participating in one of our 401(k) plans, Ms. S, was very concerned that she was going to have to sacrifice her comfort in retirement (which was about fifteen years away).

Her husband had died recently so hers was now a single-income household; she was helping her teenager and college age children with their expenses, paying down some household debt, and investing as much as she could afford in the workplace 401(k) in order to get the company match…but she was pretty sure she wasn't on track for a comfortable retirement.

We produced a retirement analysis for Ms. S, assuming moderate investment growth based on her description of her risk tolerance as "5-6 on a scale of 1-10" (and a risk tolerance assessment quiz which confirmed this).

The results of the analysis showed that Ms. S was indeed not on track.

We explained that she had three options: save more, reduce her projected retirement spending needs, or seek more growth on her investments.

She was already saving as much as she could, and she was already assuming a modest level of retirement spending…her basic needs were simple, and her lifestyle expenses were also very modest—she enjoyed painting, gardening, reading, community service projects through her church, and some short-distance travel to visit family. There was just not any wiggle room on the saving or spending sides of the equation.

We talked at length about the subject of risk tolerance, the importance of being able to sleep at night without worrying about stock market fluctuations, but also the fact that stock markets do provide growth potential—and the fact that she wouldn't need to touch her 401(k) account for another fifteen years.

We shared our Recession Reserve™ concept, which Ms. S understood might allow her to come closer to meeting her goals. We re-ran the retirement analysis with more aggressive investment growth assumptions, and sure enough the results were more favorable this time.

Ms. S decided to change her 401(k) holdings to a more aggressive allocation. She understood that this would likely mean more fluctuations in her account value, especially during recessions. She also understood that we could revisit this any time, and when she was within a few years of retiring we would start moving her back toward a more moderate mix in order to protect the money she would need for retirement expenses.

This was reassuring to Ms. S…in fact she could perhaps sleep even better now than before because with this plan in place, she could actually worry less about the stock market "roller coaster"—and also worry less about her long-term financial picture.

So the Recession Reserve™ strategy may help steady your emotional reaction to market dips, and allow you to participate more in the growth potential of the capital markets if you wish...instead of allocating your portfolio based merely on your age, or based on worries about inevitable market swings.

This can really work, but always coordinate with your investment advisor to choose efficient investments—and to find the right balance between what the math says you *can* do, and what your gut says you *should* do to sleep well at night. And be sure to reevaluate each year to make sure your Recession Reserve™ is adequate.

"Sequence Of Returns" Danger

If you put money in a stock market investment, you understand some years the markets will go up, some years it will go down, and some years will be flat or nearly flat.

For example let's say we invest $400,000 for 16 years in a hypothetical account, and take no withdrawals (please call us now if you'd really like to do that!):

Scenario 1

Age	Annual Growth	Year-End Value
50	-9.1%	$363,600
51	-11.9%	$320,368
52	-22.1%	$249,567
53	28.7%	$321,167
54	10.9%	$356,110
55	4.9%	$373,595
56	15.8%	$432,586
57	5.5%	$456,335
58	-37.0%	$287,491
59	26.5%	$363,561
60	15.1%	$418,314
61	2.1%	$427,098
62	16.0%	$495,434
63	32.4%	$655,905
64	13.7%	$745,698
65	1.4%	*$755,989*
	5.8% average	

Hypothetical returns, not reflective of a particular investment.

Scenario 2

Age	Annual Growth	Year-End Value
50	1.4%	$405,520
51	13.7%	$461,036
52	32.4%	$610,365
53	16.0%	$708,024
54	2.1%	$722,892
55	15.1%	$831,760
56	26.5%	$1,051,843
57	-37.0%	$662,661
58	5.5%	$699,041
59	15.8%	$809,420
60	4.9%	$849,162
61	10.9%	$941,551
62	28.7%	$1,211,682
63	-22.1%	$943,901
64	-11.9%	$831,671
65	-9.1%	*$755,989*
	5.8% average	

Hypothetical returns, not reflective of a particular investment.

The difference between the two boxes above is the sequence of "up" and "down" years...the "annual growth" column in scenario 2 is exactly the opposite of scenario 1, simply flipped upside down.

The average growth per year is 5.8% in both cases, and the result after sixteen years is identical: $755,989.

You could scramble those annual growth numbers any way you want—the average would still be 5.8%, and the resulting sum of money after sixteen years would be the same.

The sequence of returns doesn't matter in these scenarios.

Now let's start with $400,000 again, but this time let's assume we're starting retirement.

We'll use the same annual growth rates as scenario 1 above.

Let's assume we have $3,800 of expenses per month, part of which is covered by $2,000 per month Social Security—and we'll cover the rest by taking withdrawals from our hypothetical account.

We'll also assume we need to keep up with 3% annual inflation on our expenses, and Social Security likewise will increase 3% per year.

Here's the result.

Age	Annual Growth	Year-End Value
66	1.4%	$383,920
67	13.7%	$414,231
68	32.4%	$525,485
69	16.0%	$585,959
70	2.1%	$573,953
71	15.1%	$635,350
72	26.5%	$777,672
73	-37.0%	$463,368
74	5.5%	$461,445
75	15.8%	$506,124
76	4.9%	$501,946
77	10.9%	$526,659
78	28.7%	$646,960
79	-22.1%	$472,262
80	-11.9%	$383,438
81	-9.1%	*$314,893*
	5.8% average	

Hypothetical returns, not reflective of a particular investment.

Again, 5.8% average market returns, and at age 81 we have $314,893 remaining of our original $400,000. Not bad.

Now let's flip the order of those market returns upside down once again…simply reversing the sequence of returns…

The market average is still 5.8%.

But look at the bottom of the far right column. We ran out of money after just fourteen years.

Why?

Because if you have the bad luck of retiring during a market downturn, and withdraw a particular amount of money as planned, you will be taking a larger percentage of the account that year than if the markets happened to be up.

Age	Annual Growth	Year-End Value
66	-9.1%	$342,000
67	-11.9%	$279,088
68	-22.1%	$194,494
69	28.7%	$226,692
70	10.9%	$227,045
71	4.9%	$213,152
72	15.8%	$221,018
73	5.5%	$206,585
74	-37.0%	$102,787
75	26.5%	$101,801
76	15.1%	$88,104
77	2.1%	$60,055
78	16.0%	$38,867
79	32.4%	$19,736
80	13.7%	$0
81	1.4%	$0
	5.8% average	

Hypothetical returns, not reflective of a particular investment.

So now there is less remaining in the account to grow when markets recover; meanwhile you continue taking withdrawals, and the account is in a desperate game of "compounding catch-up" which may or may not work out in the long run. The worse the markets perform in the early years, the worse the problem may be.

On the other hand, if markets perform well the year you start your withdrawals, you'll have a better result that first year…perhaps your account grows more than you withdrew, or just keeps up, or at least drops less than it would if markets were poor. So it's in better shape at the end of the year than if the markets had dropped (or stayed flat).

If the markets are up again the second year, again you're in better shape than if the markets were down or flat.

So the better the markets do in the early years of regular withdrawals, potentially the better the long-term outcome. The worse the markets do in those early years of withdrawals, potentially the worse (or even disastrous) the outcome may be.

This is true even if the long-term yearly *average* growth percentage is identical.

Try this with any set of numbers, it's just a mathematical reality: the sequence of market returns matters greatly if you're withdrawing money from an account, and if you have the misfortune of retiring during an extended market downturn you could be in trouble.

(The sequence of returns also matters if you're *adding* money to an account—see the discussion of "dollar cost averaging" in the "Be A Disciplined Investor" section of this chapter.)

By the way, the sequence of returns in the last example, the one where we ran out of money, is the 2000-2015 total return performance of the S&P 500 index—an unmanaged index generally representative of large companies in the U.S. stock market. You can't invest directly in a benchmark index such as the S&P 500, but many investment funds do attempt to track the performance of such benchmarks. So our example may not be too far from reality for many investors during that rough market period…maybe you were one of them.

So how do you plan for the possibility that your retirement will come at another "wrong" time for the stock market?

You could adjust your withdrawals when markets are down, in order to reduce the negative effect on your account balance. But this may be painful if you're unable to meet your basic budget needs, or take trips you planned, or proceed with other lifestyle expenditures.

An alternative would be our Recession Reserve™ allocation concept. See the "What Is Your Recession Reserve™?" section for an explanation of this approach.

Another solution might be to generate income using preferred stocks or other dividend-paying stocks, laddered bonds, income riders on annuities, one or more real estate investment trust (REIT) programs, or other products specifically designed to produce cash distributions.

Some of these products may include guarantees that the income won't change (and of course the guarantees are only as good as the companies issuing them, so shop carefully with the assistance of a professional); others may still be affected by market fluctuations to some degree. So make sure your advisor helps you understand how any given income product works…including the fee structure, and whether there are provisions limiting liquidity, including penalties for excess withdrawals. See the "Income-Producing Investments" section for more information.

Be A Disciplined Investor

One of the advantages of working with a competent and experienced financial advisor is that they can help you stay on track with your investment strategy, and help you think through the pros and cons of making changes. Here are a few basic principles of disciplined investing:

> **Dollar cost averaging:** This is a simple technique that can give your investments a boost by taking advantage of the fact that any given dollar will buy more of an investment when prices drop, and less when prices rise. Just steadily add money—for example a set dollar amount each paycheck or each month—and the math takes care of the rest.
>
> Let's say Gary adds $100 each week to a hypothetical investment fund which costs $10 per share this week…so his $100 buys 10 shares.
>
> Next week if the price drops to $9 per share, Gary's $100 buys more shares: 11.11 shares. So he bought more shares when the

price was lower. That's good.

If on the third week the price goes up to $11 per share, that same $100 buys fewer shares: 9.09 shares. So he bought fewer shares when the price was higher. That's also good.

The average price per share over those three weeks was $10, right? ($9, $10, and $11 per share = $10 average).

But Gary paid $300 for a total of 30.2 shares, which is an average of $9.93 per share. So he paid a lower-than-average price per share. That's fantastic!

(If instead of buying $100 worth each week he had simply purchased ten shares each week, he would have paid $10 per share—$300 for 30 shares. That's just sad.)

As long as market prices bounce around somewhat, with a long-term upward trend (which markets tend to do over longer periods), "dollar cost averaging" helps you potentially pay less per share, own more shares, and reap the extra profit when you sell later.

NOTE: Dollar cost averaging does not assure a profit and does not protect against a loss in declining markets. This strategy involves continuous investing; you should consider your financial ability to continue purchases no matter how prices fluctuate.

Hold tight when markets are volatile (except for rebalancing): Market corrections (drops of 10% or more), smaller dips, and full-on recessions are a natural part of capital market cycles. Getting nervous during these inevitable downturns may also be natural, but taking the drastic step of selling off your shares, thus *locking in* losses, is the opposite of a sensible long-term strategy.

This isn't to say it's never ok to sell when an investment is down...but if your portfolio is properly diversified, "selling low" is rarely advisable (see exception later in this chapter). Just remind yourself that capitalism historically produces profits over the long term, and your market investments will participate in that growth potential over the long term if you let the markets do their job and don't get spooked by short-term volatility.

BUT: periodic rebalancing of investments is necessary as market changes cause your allocations to "drift." Many advisors rebalance quarterly or annually, but proactively rebalancing when markets are volatile may give you an edge. When stocks are down, rebalancing means selling some bond funds and buying stock funds—at a lower price than usual (buy low, sell high, right?). If instead stocks have nice run-up, rebalancing means capturing some of those gains and rebalancing into bond funds, thus "locking in" those gains.

Don't "chase returns": it's easy to find stocks, mutual funds, market sectors, and market styles which beat the overall market average last year. Moving your money into those investments now may or may not result in similar superior performance this year, but over the long run it's true that "past performance does not guarantee future results"...and the transaction costs of "chasing returns" may needlessly erode your investment performance.

Instead build a well-diversified portfolio which matches your risk tolerance, and let the capital markets do the rest. Don't get distracted from your strategy by someone showing you last year's (or last five years'!) "hot" investment and implying that you can expect to beat the markets with their fund or stock picks on an ongoing basis. This is a common technique used by some industry professionals to lure you away from what may be a perfectly sensible portfolio (and/or your current advisor), so take such advice with a healthy dose of salt.

Ignore the media gurus: Avoid the temptation to chase "hot" stocks you hear about from TV, radio, and magazine gurus—and ignore their dire predictions of market crashes based on the news of the day, upcoming Presidential elections, market patterns, or their proprietary market-prediction formula.

A 2012 study by CXO Advisory Group looked at 6,582 predictions by 68 of these media "experts" from 2005 - 2012 and found their success rate to be about 47%...*worse* than flipping coins! And by the time you get to the phone or the internet to make a purchase of a "hot" stock, the price may have already spiked (ironically in some cases *because* of the TV guru's comments), so you may suffer a loss when the price drops back to normal.

One of our favorite clients, Mrs. G, likes to take trips to nearby casinos with her little gang of retired ladies for some light gambling. She calls us about once a year to ask if she should invest in a new (or existing) stock she heard good things about on a market news TV show. Our answer is always the same...a recap of the previous paragraph.

Now of course those TV tips do pan out sometimes, and Mrs. G doesn't let us forget it—but we never regret advising her to stick with a diversified portfolio, which has done well for her over time. And anyway, in many cases those "hot" stocks are already included in one of her funds, with about the weight they've *earned* in the capital markets.

As for predictions of market drops, corrections, and recessions: any given day plenty of people make predictions, and eventually some of them will be correct because markets do vary, and recessions do happen...but no one has ever consistently predicted the markets over the long run. Ever. Market timing just doesn't work, and in fact over time may erode your investment growth potential. Ironically, the losses people take trying to avoid another 2008 are often worse than 2008!

Instead, always assume the next recession will start tomorrow, because it may. Allocate investments based on your risk tolerance as we've discussed in previous sections, so when markets drop you can remind yourself that you've already prepared for it—so there's no reason to panic. (See "What's Your Recession Reserve™?" section for a sensible approach.)

Invest Efficiently

"Mutual funds" and "exchange traded funds" (ETF's) are baskets of dozens, hundreds, or thousands of stocks and/or bonds. Many investment advisors use these "pooled" funds in client portfolios.

"Active" mutual fund managers (individuals or teams working for fund companies) buy and sell securities, trying to match or beat the performance of the overall stock, bond, and alternatives markets. Their performance is judged against their "benchmark index"—a large representative sample of their segment of the market such as large U.S. companies (the S&P 500 index, Russell 1000 index, Dow Industrials, and others), small companies (Russell 2000 index, S&P SmallCap 600 index, and others), international companies (FTSE index and others), bonds (Barclays index and others), and so on.

Every year, the Standard And Poor's organization conducts a broad review of U.S. mutual fund performance. The study is called S&P Indices Versus Active, or SPIVA, and it gauges just how good these professional stock pickers are at outsmarting the markets.

Consistently, year after year, the results show that the markets are efficient—meaning that stock prices adjust quickly to account for relevant new information, which in our modern age of instant communication is available to all investors simultaneously.

Therefore in any given year some fund managers do beat the

market, but it's not the same managers from year to year. You can't predict which ones it will be this year… and ultimately, **over the long run, fund managers tend to perform about average, minus their expenses and trading costs.**

It's not too hard to find the "expense ratio" percentage in your fund prospectus; multiply the amount you have invested by that percentage and this is your annual cost just to own the fund. This pays for the fund managers' salaries and their analysts, marketing costs, and other overhead expenses.

Trading costs create an additional drag on your performance, but are nowhere to be found in the prospectus—fund companies are not required to report those at all. They're only required to report the "turnover ratio" (percentage), which reflects the amount of the fund's trading activity: 100% turnover would mean that over the course of the last year, every stock and/or bond was sold, and a replacement purchased. The cost of each trade involves three elements: 1) a sales commission; 2) the "bid-ask" spread (the difference between what buyers will pay and sellers will accept); and 3) potentially a "market impact" cost—where buying or selling a large quantity of a stock or bonds moves the price of the stock or bond: if they buy a large quantity, it can drive up the price paid; if they sell a large quantity, it can drive down the price received…*exactly the opposite of what you want as the investor.*

Fortunately there are studies to help estimate the costs. A 2013 university study called "Shedding Light On Invisible Costs: Trading Costs And Mutual Fund Performance" (Edelen, Evans, Kadlec) examined each trade inside 1,758 U.S. mutual funds from 1996 – 2006 (almost every U.S. mutual fund!), and estimated an average turnover cost to investors of 1.44% per year. However the cost varied depending on the style and size of each fund examined, ranging from .61% to 3.17%.

A simpler rule of thumb is from a 1998 research paper ("The Official Icebergs of Transaction Costs," Commentary #54, Plexus Group): for every 100% of turnover, assume about 1.16% cost. In our own analyses of investor portfolios, due to the weighting of the styles of funds in most portfolio allocations we have found that this method comes surprisingly close to the same result as when we use 2013 study's numbers for comparison.

So if a mutual fund turnover ratio is 60%, multiply 60 x 1.16% = 0.696% estimated turnover expense. So a $100,000 portfolio x 0.696% = $696 estimated trading costs per year. Again it's important to understand that the actual trading costs are not available to investors so we can only make this rough educated guess.

Now you might think the trading activity of mutual fund managers would result in better performance despite the costs—after all, they're the experts, and if they buy or sell a stock, they could tell you why they think it's a good idea. However that same 2013 study found higher-turnover funds perform an average of 1.92% *worse* than lower-turnover funds. The study found the less trading, the better the performance. Read that sentence again and let it sink in.

Why? Because markets are efficient, fund managers can't consistently predict what markets will do, and they can't even consistently predict whether any given stock will go up or down. So their expensive trading activity is like a boat anchor, potentially dragging down your investment performance.

Because of this eye-opening research, many of our clients prefer mutual funds and ETF's with lower-than-average costs, including lower-than-average turnover. This approach may include "passive index fund" portfolios. Instead of having a manager trying to match or beat their benchmark, an index fund simply mirrors a benchmark index…owning all the same securities that make up the index, or a large representative sample. The goal is to track the overall market, not to beat it. The investment costs and turnover tend to be very low, meaning potentially more money stays in the account, working for the client.

There are additional advantages to this approach. Lower

turnover investments generate less capital gains taxes, an important consideration in taxable (non-IRA) accounts. Also, active managers may keep excessive cash handy in a fund so they can hop on "hot" stocks. Cash does not perform well in an investment—this is known as "cash drag." Comparatively, index funds need very little cash on hand.

Of course there's one more piece to the investment cost puzzle: the fees you pay your investment advisor. They're the gatekeeper you want to steer you toward good investments, but their fees should be reasonable. Ask your advisor about your market investment costs and turnover—and look at your investments to see the relationship between lower costs and better performance potential.

Way Too Much Of A Good Thing…

There's a well-known auto parts company headquartered in our town which started very small, and has been an amazing success story.

Some of our clients were purchasing stock shares in this company before we ever met them, and now those shares have grown in value so dramatically that these folks are amazed and delighted.

And they potentially have a couple of serious problems.

Don't get us wrong, we're very happy for them, and perhaps even a bit jealous! But…

First, some of them now have what's known as a "concentrated portfolio": too many eggs in one basket, which exposes them to serious risks (see "Investment Risk And Your Risk Tolerance" section), including the risk that they could lose some or even all of the value of that stock if the company runs into trouble.

Now we have absolutely no reason to think that company and its stock value won't continue to grow…but having more than about 5% of your portfolio exposed to any one company stock is not advisable as a general rule. Ask anyone who owned Enron stock, or WorldCom, or any of hundreds of companies which have defaulted over the years.

The other potential problem is capital gains tax, which we discuss in the "Tax Efficiency" section below.

Investment Tax Efficiency: 401(k)'s, 403(b)'s, IRA's…And "Non-Qualified" Investments

Investors and their advisors have a certain amount of control over their tax picture. Here are the basics.

Tax-deferred accounts: You don't pay tax on the money until you withdraw it in retirement. If you withdraw before age 59 ½, you may owe an IRS penalty in addition to tax, except when the money is used for certain situations (visit IRS.gov for the current list of exceptions). Here are examples:

- **The triple-crown tax advantage: company-sponsored retirement plans such as 401(k)'s, 4013(b)'s, Simple IRA's, SEP's, and others:** your employer withholds part of your pay before taxes are taken out, and sends the money to an investment company who allocates it to investment funds you select. The tax burden on your paycheck is reduced, but your take-home budget is only reduced by the net amount you *would have* taken home *after* taxes.

    The money you would have taken home *plus* the amount that would have gone to the government is instead put to work in your retirement account, so you are saving more than you might otherwise... and the money grows tax-deferred in your account until withdrawn.

At that point, many retirees may be in a lower tax bracket than they were in their high-earning year—so when they finally do have to pay tax it may be at a significantly lower tax rate. We call all this a "triple-crown" tax advantage.

- **IRA (individual retirement account/arrangement):**

    Traditional IRA: This is an individually-owned account which works similarly to a workplace retirement plan—you can tax-deduct contributions and pay no tax on that income until you withdraw money in retirement. The contribution limits often change from year to year (indexed by Congress to go up over time), so check with your tax or financial advisor for the current year's rules.

    Roth IRA: This allows you to contribute *after-tax* ("take-home") money, and the subsequent *growth* is State and Federal income tax-free as long as you don't make withdrawals for a period of time after opening the account—check with your tax professional for current rules.

    A Roth IRA may be appropriate if (1) you expect to be in a higher tax bracket after retirement than you're in now, for example if you're currently in a low tax bracket because you're in the early stages of your career; and/or (2) you expect Congress to raise tax rates significantly in the future.

    In either case you could be better off to pay the tax now rather than in the future; on the other hand this choice requires you to make certain assumptions about your future tax picture which may or may not pan out. Work with your financial planning professional and tax advisor to think through the pros and cons of a Roth IRA for your own situation.

> **Roth conversion:** IRS rules allow you to pay the tax on part or all of a tax-deferred IRA account and convert it to a Roth IRA. It makes no sense to use IRA funds to pay the tax, so you need to have surplus non-IRA funds available for that.
>
> The amount of the IRA conversion will be seen by the IRS as taxable income for the year of the conversion, so ironically you could drive yourself into a tax problem if you're not careful…work with your tax professional to decide whether to do a Roth conversion.

- **Annuities:** For a "non-qualified" (non-IRA) annuity, tax on growth is deferred until you make withdrawals. This tax deferral feature can make an annuity an attractive option from a tax management standpoint.

  When you take withdrawals from an annuity, the growth comes out first and is taxed as ordinary income; subsequent withdrawals of your original principal are not taxed at all because you used after-tax money to start with.

  An annuity may be held within a traditional IRA account. In this case the tax-deferral benefits of an annuity don't add any value because a traditional IRA is already tax deferred…but there may be other reasons an annuity could make sense for a particular IRA. Of course *all* withdrawals from an IRA are taxable, not just the growth.

If an annuity is held as a Roth IRA, it's treated as usual for a Roth: no tax on withdrawals, as long as the Roth IRA was held for at least five years.

Important: tax laws change frequently, so make sure your tax and financial advisor help you stay up-to-date to help avoid potential problems.

Investments that may be held in either tax-deferred or taxable accounts:

- **Bank products:** CD's, savings accounts, and money market accounts: even if interest is automatically reinvested, it's considered taxable. So you'll receive a 1099 form from the bank which you must report on your tax returns.

    Holding bank products inside an IRA can defer taxation until you make withdrawals in retirement; Roth IRA's are completely State and Federal tax-free if you meet certain requirements. Work with your tax professional to understand the rules, and your options.

- **Mutual funds:** If a mutual fund trades one of its holdings (a stock or bond for example) and there is a gain, the fund is required to distribute most of the gains to shareholders.

    If the mutual fund is held in an account that is tax deferred, such as an IRA, workplace retirement account, or annuity, this is not a taxable event for the investor.

    But if the fund is held in a taxable account, the investor will receive an IRS 1099 form and may owe taxes, even if the proceeds were automatically reinvested.

Actively managed mutual funds, where stocks may be frequently traded, generally tend to generate more capital gains taxation than index funds which generally trade less frequently.

Exchange traded funds (ETF's), unlike mutual funds, are *not* required to distribute capital gains. So an index ETF may be more tax efficient compared to other options. See discussions elsewhere in this chapter for more information about the advantages of index funds.

Capital Gains Are Great! Capital Gains Tax, Not So Much

A couple who came to one of our public workshops and met with us in our office later had seen their non-IRA account grow from $800,000 to $1.2 million *in just one year* thanks to a single holding of a stock which had grown dramatically (that auto parts store stock we mentioned elsewhere).

They knew they should diversify, but if they sold most of that stock now, they would be looking at a huge capital gains tax bill. It's a nice problem to have—paying tax on a large gain still leaves you a profit!

So this couple has three choices:

1. Sell enough of the stock to "correctly" diversify the portfolio, and pay potentially significant capital gains tax.

2. Work with their tax accountant to "crawl out" of this holding over a period of time.

At the time of this writing, the capital gains tax rate is *zero* for taxpayers whose adjusted gross income (AGI) is below a certain threshold. In such a tax environment, they might want to work with their advisors to calculate the amount of capital gains they can absorb before significant taxation applies, and take just that amount of gains; then perform the same calculation each of the next few years until they've reduced their exposure to that stock to the desired amount.

3. Continue to hold the stock and earmark it for heirs—because heirs will receive a "stepped-up basis" (no capital gains tax, and a fresh starting value upon which taxable gains can build). If the stock value holds up, or continues to increase, this may turn out to be a sensible strategy.

However this client has about 50% of their account in a single stock now; we're very happy for their investing success and hate to rain on their parade, but as trusted advisors we must remind them of the critical importance of diversification.

Now when we advised this client of the peril presented by their overexposure to this one stock, their response was, "We know. But we never expected this much growth from one stock, and we don't need anywhere near that much money to meet our retirement needs, so we're letting it ride.

"Worst case, that stock tanks, but our kids' inheritance will still be what we planned years ago from our other holdings. Best case, it will be a huge bonus for them. And besides, it's fun to watch this stock. It's worth the risk to us…and we've watched that company, and how they treat their employees, and how they give back to the community, and we think it's a good bet that they'll continue to be successful."

These clients chose to hold steady for now. In the end it's your football, and your football field—our job as advisors is to help you think through the opportunities and risks to make an informed decision.

When Is Selling Low A Good Thing?

In a taxable account, when you sell a stock or fund which has grown in value, you may owe capital gains tax on the profit. But if you can harvest those gains when they're as low as possible, such as in a market downturn, and then buy a replacement—perhaps even buying the same holding (but within IRS "wash sale" rules requiring a specific amount of time between transactions)—it can be like hitting the capital gains "reset" button.

Work with your advisor on this technique—in some years, the capital gains rate has been zero if adjusted gross income is below a certain threshold, potentially making this an even more powerful tool.

Annuities

Annuities are insurance products with unique tax and return qualities. These tax deferred vehicles are managed by large life insurance companies; annuities may provide both growth potential and income potential.

There may be penalties for early withdrawals, and IRS penalties for withdrawals before age 59 ½. There may also be liquidity limits and other provisions. Make sure you review your prospectus for variable annuities, and understand fees (if any).

All Annuities Have These Advantages…

1. **Tax deferral:** Growth is not taxed until pulled out. This is an advantage for taxable accounts—accounts which are not already in a tax-deferred IRA or 401(k) for example (however other features of annuities may still be attractive for an IRA account, even though there's no difference from a tax perspective).

2. **Growth potential:** There are three methods, explained below.

3. **Income potential:** Again there are a few different ways this can be structured, explained below.

4. **Backed by large insurance companies:** Highly rated insurance companies have a far lower rate of default than banks in most years, partly due to much larger cash reserve requirements for insurance companies. Not that banks are unsafe either—in either case accounts are backed up to a certain limit by legally-required reimbursement systems (the FDIC for banks, and State Guaranty Associations for annuities). Of course you should use companies which have good scores from the well-established and heavily regulated industry rating agencies…because it's true that guarantees are only as strong as the companies issuing them.

…And Some Annuities May Have These Disadvantages

1. **Holding ("surrender") period:** Most contracts (though not all) require you to leave the money alone for a period of time. There may or may not be provisions for partial penalty-free withdrawals, or exceptions for certain situations such as terminal illness diagnosis or a nursing home stay; beyond that, any "excess" withdrawals may be subject to a penalty. These holding periods are sort of a "time price" you pay in exchange for benefits you may find attractive.

2. **Some are expensive:** "Variable annuities" (explained below) typically have a base contract fee, fees for underlying investments, and fees for optional income riders or optional enhanced death benefit features.

    "Fixed annuities" generally have no fees—they are not in the stock market and there is no option for an income rider.

"Indexed annuities" typically don't have fees for the base contract, but may have a fee for an optional income rider; there are typically no investment fees because the money is not in the stock market.

3. **Some are complicated:** This depends on the contract—and just because something is complicated doesn't necessarily mean it's bad. Just make sure your advisor does a good job explaining it to you, and if you don't understand it, don't proceed. Fixed annuities are generally very simple. Indexed annuities may have a simple or complicated method of crediting interest, and a simple or complicated optional income rider. Variable annuities may also have simple or complicated income riders and/or growth formulas. Use products that best meet your needs, and take the time to understand them.

The Four Types Of Annuities

1. **Income-Only Annuity With Annuitization (also known as "immediate annuity" or "single premium deferred immediate annuity"):** Annuities were originally designed (a couple of thousand years ago) as strictly income products, and these still exist: you hand over a lump sum of money to the insurance company, and it is converted into a steady income stream for a certain period of time, or for the lifetime of the "annuitant"...a process called "annuitization."

This means kissing your original lump sum goodbye in exchange for the income guarantee.

If you die the next day, you lose that bet—your lump sum is gone, and you didn't get much income.

On the other hand if you live to age 105, you may have received far more money than that original lump sum could have reasonably been expected to generate.

This gamble was attractive in the past because it eliminated the stress of not being sure if you could make your retirement savings last...it was like insuring your retirement savings against a long lifespan, essentially creating your own "personal pension" plan. In fact company pension plans are based on a deferred (delayed) annuity structure of this type.

Although this kind of product always had a role in the financial planning marketplace, nobody liked giving up their lump sum without knowing whether the gamble would pay off.

2. **Variable Annuity (VA):** Introduced in 1952, this type of contract includes an underlying stock market investment account ("sub-account") in addition to an optional income guarantee ("income rider").

    With an income rider in place of the annuitization requirement, clients don't have to give up their lump sum in order to enjoy the income features of an annuity.

    The income rider may pay you an income stream for life (or other period), and if there is money left in the account at your death, that remaining sum goes to your heirs.

    But again, always remember a guarantee is only as good as the issuing company—so use highly rated companies.

    Modern variable annuities may have a wide variety of investment options for the sub-accounts; these investments are much like mutual funds—baskets of stocks and/or bonds which may either be actively managed, or passive index funds.

    The investment sub-account will have fees, as will the optional income rider, and the basic contract usually also has a fee. So variable annuities can be expensive, but may fulfil a role for your financial planning needs, especially if guaranteed income appeals to you and you're an aggressive investor (more aggressive investments may have better potential to overcome the fees, while the growth of conservative investments in a variable annuity may not keep up).

Work with your advisor to understand whether a variable annuity makes sense for your situation and for your risk tolerance. Remember all optional benefits such as riders and bonuses often mean an additional cost. The guarantees associated with optional benefits are backed by (and subject to the claims-paying ability of) the issuing insurance company.

3. **Equity Indexed Annuity (EIA; may also be called Fixed Indexed Annuity or FIA):** With this type of annuity your money is not invested directly in the stock market. Instead, conservative growth potential comes in the form of interest credited to your account based on the performance of a stock market index such as the S&P 500 (a well-known measure of the performance of the large-companies segment of the U.S. stock market). Not all contracts use the S&P 500 benchmark, but for the ones that do:

>If the S&P 500 is up for the year, you receive part of the gains.

>If the S&P 500 is down for the year, you don't gain, and you don't lose.

There are many different variations on how gains are credited—and limited. The most popular type of limits as of this writing are "caps" and "participation rates."

>**Example 1:** 5% cap: if the S&P 500 is up 3% since your last contract anniversary, you get 3% credited to your account; if the S&P 500 is up 12%, you get 5% (no

more than the cap in other words); if the S&P 500 is down, you get 0%.

Example 2: participation rate 50%: if the S&P 500 is up 10% you get 5%; if the S&P 500 is up 30% you get 15%. And as with most indexed annuity contracts, if the S&P 500 is down for the year, you get 0%.

When you look at actual stock market performance from year to year, you can see how eliminating the "down" years can potentially provide a decent interest rate even if you just get a portion of each "up" year.

Since fees tend to be much lower (or non-existent) in indexed annuities, this may be a better option than the variable annuity for many conservative investors.

Indexed annuities are also required to include a minimal guaranteed rate of return in case markets go down and stay down. However any such guarantee is subject to the claims-paying ability of the issuing insurance company. And if the minimum guarantee is based on anything less than the full amount of money you put in, you could potentially still lose money in such a "permanent down-market" scenario if you don't leave the money in the contract long enough.

An indexed annuity may include an optional income rider, which usually includes an annual fee. Your income is distributed from your account balance, and if there's money left over when you die, it goes to your beneficiaries. What if the income totally depletes the account before you die? The company has agreed contractually to continue paying you the income, no matter how long you live, *even if the account balance drops all the way to zero.*

A basic indexed annuity contract normally has no fees other than the optional income rider, so if you don't choose to include an income rider, you may pay no fees at all.

Each equity indexed annuity company is required by law to be a member of its State Guaranty Association—a pooled fund to protect clients' accounts up to a certain limit in the event of company default (similar to the FDIC for banks).

However due to the large cash reserve requirements and other regulations on annuity companies, company defaults are relatively rare…much less common than banks in most years. Still, it's important to work with your advisor and use highly-rated, solid companies.

4. **Fixed Annuity:** This is a relatively simple product which pays a fixed interest rate, with no income rider option. You could still annuitize if you like at any point, but it's not required. There are typically no fees.

Performance is usually somewhat better than bank CD's, but generally less growth-oriented than indexed annuities or variable annuities. This is a conservative option with conservative growth potential.

Income-Producing Investments (And Their Tax Ramifications)

The following investments may produce income, growth potential, or both. However, many of these sources of income do not come with guarantees, and for the ones that do, the guarantees are only as good as the companies issuing them. As always, past performance does not guarantee future results. So work with a qualified and experienced investment advisor to understand the potential risks and rewards of each, their tax ramifications, and how they might (or might not) fit your planning needs.

Bank products: CD's, savings accounts, and money market accounts generally pay a fixed interest rate for a period of time, and the interest can be used as an income source. In a typical interest rate environment this may be workable; in a very low interest rate environment such as the extended low-interest period following the 2008 recession, income may be minimal.

Interest is taxable as ordinary income whether you have it automatically reinvested or distributed as income.

Market gains: If a stock or stock fund (or anything else of value you own) increases in value and you sell it, that "capital gain" may either be reinvested or used for income.

You may also sell market investments periodically and use the cash for your basic needs or lifestyle needs, in which case the proceeds may or may not include capital gains. For example if markets are down, you may be withdrawing principal instead of gains, thus potentially depleting your original investment.

A qualified advisor can help you potentially avoid selling at a loss...for example we use our Recession Reserve™ process for our clients to try to reduce or avoid such losses in their stock and bond portfolios (see "What's Your Recession Reserve™?" section of the Investing chapter).

During most historical periods, capital gains have been taxed at a lower rate than ordinary income in an attempt by Congress to encourage investing in capital markets. Ask your tax professional and/or financial advisor for details about the current tax environment for capital gains.

Income annuities: See a general discussion of annuities in the previous section.

>**Annuitization:** You give up your principal in order to receive an income stream (known as "annuitization").

>**Income rider:** Guarantees an income stream, for life or

for some other period, and the income is deducted from the account balance—but if there is money left in the account when you die, it goes to your surviving spouse or other heirs. An income rider usually has a fee which is deducted from your account balance. Always remember that the guarantees of an annuity are only as good as the issuing company.

One of our clients, Mrs. H, retired from Ford and had grave concerns about the strength of the company and the pension plan she was offered...and she knew that if she and her husband died prematurely there would be nothing for her adult children to inherit from the pension plan.

Ford offered Mrs. H a monetary lump sum instead of a monthly pension payment, and she preferred this option even though in this case we couldn't convert the lump sum to as much guaranteed income as the pension plan would have paid—at least not right away.

We found an indexed annuity with an income rider which, if Mrs. H deferred the start of the annuity income payments for a couple of years, would generate enough income to meet her living expenses.

So Mrs. H and Mr. H were both able to sleep better at night and had a better shot at leaving an inheritance.

In other cases, clients prefer the company pension payments over the lump sum. Work with your advisor to understand the pros and cons of each approach.

Bonds: A bond is essentially a loan—you hand over money to a company or government, they hand you the bond. You hold the bond for a specific period of time, and the bond issuer pays you interest during that time. At the end of the time period, they give you back your original investment. There are variations on this theme, but this is the basic idea.

The longer the time period, and the bigger the risk that the company or government will default on their debt to you, the higher the interest rate they'll pay in general. For example a high-yield or "junk" bond often pays high interest rates to investors because they have a higher probability of default in the opinion of bond rating agencies; on the other hand a U.S. government bond is generally considered to be very high quality, with very low risk of default, so it may pay relatively low interest.

You can buy a series of bonds with staggered end dates; as each one ends, you buy another, so the result is a steady (or relatively steady) flow of income over time. This is called a "bond ladder."

A municipal bond (issued by a city or state) produces interest that is exempt from Federal tax. This is one way to help manage the tax burden of a taxable (non-IRA) account.

If you buy a bond fund instead of individual bonds, the bond fund manager does the laddering for you, buying tens or hundreds or even thousands of bonds (or with exchange traded funds the process is essentially automated).

With a bond fund, the interest can either be distributed to you as income, or automatically reinvested for conservative growth potential.

Bond funds are generally more stable than stock funds, so in addition to potentially producing income they are also commonly used in investment portfolios to provide some cushion against stock market volatility…as the conservative half of a moderate portfolio for example.

One very important factor to consider when purchasing bonds or bond funds is that bond values are related to interest rates in the general economy in an inverse (opposite) way: when interest rates rise, prices for existing bonds tend to fall; and when interest rates drop, prices for existing bonds tend to rise.

Imagine you purchase a bond for $1,000 which pays 3% interest, but the following year a new $1,000 bond of the same quality is available which pays 4% interest. How much will someone pay for your 3% bond now if you want to sell it? Obviously it will be less than the $1,000 you paid for it. (There is a formula to find the break-even sale price, and that would be the new "fair market" price.)

On the other hand if interest rates for similar new bonds drop from 3% to 2%, you may receive more for your 3% bond than the $1,000 you paid for it.

The longer-term the bond, the bigger this effect may become, whichever way interest rates go. So in a very low interest rate environment, it may make sense to stick with short- to mid-term bonds in anticipation of interest rates eventually rising. In a very high interest rate environment, it may make sense to consider longer term bonds. This isn't market timing—the Federal Reserve seeks a moderate interest rate and will adjust the money supply in order to achieve that goal when economic conditions allow. So if rates are unusually high or low, it's likely that rates will eventually return to "normal."

Stock dividends: If you own stock in a company, the company may distribute profits to shareholders periodically in the form of dividends. You may have dividends reinvested automatically, or distributed to you as cash income.

"Preferred stocks" behave somewhat like a hybrid between stocks and bonds, typically with higher and steadier dividends than common stocks...but often at the expense of lower growth potential. Work with your advisor to understand the pros and cons of preferred stocks, as they have unique risk and reward characteristics.

Taxation of dividends may depend on the type and location of companies issuing the dividends...those which meet specific criteria may qualify for capital gains tax treatment.

Real estate income trust (REIT): A REIT company pools investor funds to buy real estate properties, which they then lease or rent out. Office buildings, warehouses, retail stores, and apartment buildings are common holdings.

The investors receive a portion of the ongoing rent or lease payments from tenants. This income may be distributed as income, or in some offerings may be automatically reinvested. Sometimes the REIT companies may use some of the original pool of investor money to pay distributions, or use loans or proceeds from real estate sales when tenant payments aren't sufficient to meet targets.

These are "illiquid" investments—access to your original investment may be limited or nonexistent.

After a period of time the REIT company attempts to resell the properties and return money to the investors—which may be more or less than the original investments, *or possibly none at all*, depending on the real estate market.

Alternatively, the REIT company may stage a public offering where investor shares are turned into stock shares, which investors may then trade on a public stock exchange for whatever price the markets will bear.

REIT's may involve considerable risk, and the cost of operating the REIT may detract significantly from income and growth for investors. In fact there is no guarantee a REIT will fulfill any of its provisions, so it's critical that you proceed very carefully. Work with an experienced advisor to evaluate the quality of any REIT before investing, and ask questions.

Most REIT's have minimum income and/or net worth requirements for investors.

Distributions from REIT's are treated as ordinary income for tax purposes.

Other income-focused investments:

- Business development companies ("BDC") and similar "note" programs
- Gas/oil partnership programs
- Reverse mortgage

BDC's, note programs, and gas/oil programs can potentially be good sources of income, and gas/oil partnerships may also provide certain tax advantages. However these investments are generally illiquid, and may also involve certain other risks—including the risk of loss. Work closely with a securities-licensed advisor and take the time to understand the pros and cons of these programs.

A reverse mortgage converts your equity (ownership) of your home into an income stream while you still live there; in exchange, the reverse mortgage company eventually attains ownership of the home. This may be a viable option for some consumers, especially if leaving the home to heirs is not a priority. Again, work with an experienced professional to determine whether this potential income source makes sense for your situation.

Real estate rentals: this earns its own section, see below.

Rental Real Estate: You're The Landlord!

Owning rental property can be a great way to generate primary or supplemental income if you know what you're doing (especially if you're handy enough to do some or all of your own maintenance and repairs).

If you're not experienced: proceed very carefully—owning income-generating property can be rewarding, but it can be disastrous if you get in over your head or fail to plan for problems...and the list of potential problems is long. Do your research, make sure you have good guidance before diving in, and start slowly.

Here are some basics:

It's a business. Seek continual improvement in your business practices, especially when it comes to evaluating, purchasing, and maintaining properties, screening tenants, managing cash flows, and knowing when to cut losses and get out of a particular holding. Talk to other income-property owners to gain from their experience.

Set up a business entity (for example LLC or corporation) to own your rental property—don't own it directly yourself (in other words don't set it up as "sole proprietor" ownership). This is critical to avoid having your personal assets potentially subject to seizure in the event of a legal proceeding against you.

Vet the tenants. Always (always) conduct a thorough background check on prospective tenants including a credit check—and that means each and every adult who will be occupying your property.

Don't allow one tenant to "take responsibility" for the others, because this may be difficult or impossible to enforce in court.

Check all references, and never let a prospective tenant's words, or an immediate cash offer, or anything else sway you from your established tenant evaluation process. A new tenant may be in a big hurry to move for a perfectly legitimate reason; or it may be a scam. You don't know them, so you can't assume they're honest, and you can't assume they're not. You must have a process, and you must follow it religiously, every time. An experienced tenant understands this; an inexperienced tenant needs to learn this, or rent elsewhere.

If a prospective tenant can't list at least two past landlords as references (take current landlord statements with a grain of salt, as they may paint a pretty picture just to get rid of a terrible tenant!), and two employment references: consider renting to someone else. It's worth a month or two of vacancy to avoid potentially serious, expensive, and possibly long-term problems.

A prospective tenant's monthly income should be at least three times the monthly rent.

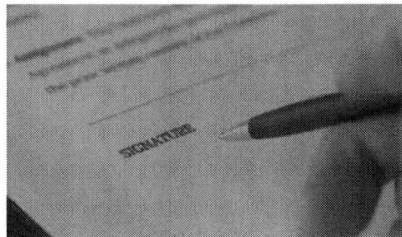

Get a signature. Provide tenants a document specifying when rent is due, rules about pets, noise, whether waterbeds are allowed (some people still do have those!), everything. Get a signature. Imagine what a judge will ask if you end up in small claims court (as claimant or defendant), and imagine what could happen if it's your word against theirs, instead of in writing. Having everything in writing could actually prevent that court appearance to begin with, because the understanding between you and your tenants is as clear as possible—legal issues live in the "gray areas" so try to eliminate as many gray areas as possible on the front end.

Enforce your rules consistently. Otherwise that imaginary future judge may determine that the real-world tenant "agreement" is different than what you put on paper.

Price rent correctly. Don't be shy about raising rents if market conditions justify it…you should check the going rate for similar nearby units on an annual basis. Failure to do so could compromise the ultimate value of your units when it comes time to sell; and you don't want to have to play catch-up at some point by suddenly raising rents significantly for existing tenants, at the risk of potentially losing them.

Get a good accountant. One who is qualified and experienced, who understands tax rules around income real estate and can help you make sure you take advantage of available exclusions and deductions. See the "Passive Activity And At-Risk Rules For Investors And Landlords" section of the Tax Management chapter for other relevant tax concepts.

The "granddaddy" of real estate tax breaks is the 1031 exchange, which allows you to defer capital gains tax when you sell a piece of property…as long as you identify and purchase a replacement property within a specific timeframe, and the replacement property is for similar use (for example selling one single-family rental unit then buying another; or selling a commercial lease property then buying another—again, get experienced professional advice to make sure you don't run afoul of the IRS).

Diversify. Diversification is as critical for property owners as for any other investor or business owner, and that doesn't just mean owning different types of real property…2008 was a wake-up call for many landlords who never imagined the values of their properties could go any direction but "up." If you're overweight to real estate in your portfolio, consider diversification into stocks, bonds, bank instruments, annuities, or alternatives which may provide growth potential and spread your risk across the broader economy.

The experience you gain in other investments will also help if and when you decided to get out of the rental business—you'll have a more realistic idea of the kind of returns and cash flow to expect from other kinds of investments, so you'll be in a better position to build a long-term plan for the transition.

Have an exit plan. The day will likely come when you no longer want to deal with the day to day demands of income real estate management. Prepare well ahead either to turn over management to others, or to get out entirely. Replacing some or all of that income stream will require a realistic examination of your options with the help of a professional investment advisor.

Speculative Investments—And Is Gold Safe Or Speculative?

"Speculative" just means "risky." This may mean the price of an investment fluctuates a lot, or maybe it's difficult to set a price to begin with—in some cases because there's a limited market (hard to find a buyer).

As with any investment, you're not guaranteed a profit when you sell, but with speculative investments that risk may be even greater. Don't purchase such investments (at least not in any significant quantity) unless you don't mind the strong possibility of losing money, or waiting a potentially long time for a sale to take place at all.

Examples of speculative investments include art, collectibles, thinly traded small- or micro-company stocks, the contraption your uncle invented in the garage and wants you to chip in to promote, and gold or other precious metals. (Yes many people mistakenly believe gold is a conservative, stable investment—but prices for gold and other precious metals are often quite volatile. It's very interesting to listen over time to radio commercials by companies who sell gold—when gold prices are down, they trumpet "buy low—buy now!" When gold prices are up, they yell, "Look what you're missing—buy now!")

Keep in mind if you buy very broad mutual funds or ETF's, for example a "total market" fund which attempts to hold a large swath of the capital markets, such a fund may already include a portion of relatively small companies, as well as some commodities holdings including precious metals. So you may already own a position in gold of approximately the size gold has *earned* in the overall investing marketplace.

Treat speculative investments as you would treat an individual company stock…a good rule of thumb is not to put more than about 5% of your portfolio into any single potentially volatile asset, including speculative investments.

Do-It-Yourself-Investor Dangers

With the availability of online services which make it relatively easy and inexpensive to manage your own investments, it may be tempting to try your hand at Wall Street. And you may have the time, energy, and talent to educate yourself to a degree that makes it possible to succeed.

However this is not to be taken lightly. You must commit to putting in the many hours required to understand what you're doing, and how you can hurt yourself financially. You must account for the many types of investment risk, and how best to manage those risks. And you need to seek information from many sources—keeping one eye on potential hidden agendas, as information from independent academic studies may be more trustworthy than information from investment companies who stand to profit from your investment decisions.

Individual investors may tend to make decisions based on emotion…when markets are up, or a particular stock is up, they get excited and buy—in other words, they "buy high." And as we've mentioned elsewhere, sometimes they may also buy or hang onto more of a single holding than is appropriate for a diversified portfolio—known as a "concentrated position"—which could expose the portfolio to excessive risk of loss.

On the other end of the spectrum, when values drop, they get worried and sell. These are natural reactions, but a losing approach to investing.

Part of the advantage of working with a professional is that they can discuss with you the pros and cons of such decisions…and perhaps save you from yourself.

Tax management of investments can also be a minefield, and again, this is where a professional advisor can help determine a course of action to potentially reduce your tax burden for capital gains tax, dividend taxes, income tax…even the percentage of your Social Security that may be subject to taxation because of actions you take with investments.

One of our clients called to say she and her husband had been reading the financial press and were curious about a particular index mutual fund a magazine was recommending. She wanted to know how to go about buying it herself, so we gave her some guidance on that.

We also let her know that a similar (but broader) index fund was already in their portfolio with us...but that we were using a "growth" version of the fund which pays a lower rate of dividends in their taxable account, therefore potentially reducing their tax burden.

Finally we mentioned that the fund they were considering covered only one part of the market—large U.S. companies—and that we include funds in their portfolio to cover other market styles as well, because you never know which will be the winner from year to year.

A couple of days later the client walked in with a check, asking that we go ahead and add it to their existing account. We're not sure if they also invested a little money on their own in the fund she was asking about, which would be perfectly fine...but they wanted the bulk of their savings managed professionally. We think that was a good call.

Special Investing Considerations For Business Owners

If you're like most entrepreneurs, your company may be your biggest asset. You've put in blood, sweat, and tears—and probably some capital along the way. And you may be plowing most or all profits right back into the business, and that's normal too.

But if you understand the risk of putting all of your savings into one publically traded stock, you should know that same risk applies to your own company. Sure you know your company books better than you may ever know the fundamentals of a publically traded stock, but that doesn't make it risk-free.

Consider diversifying across stock and bond markets in line with your investment risk tolerance, and include the equity in your own company in that calculation.

If you're in a position to implement a tax-advantaged retirement savings plan for your employees, choose a plan with your own retirement planning goals in mind as well. The amount you can invest annually may be dramatically more or less depending on which type you choose. A 401(k) typically costs more time and money to administer than a Simple IRA, but may also allow far more contributions from the business owner. Weigh pros and cons with your advisor, and use an advisor who is experienced at shopping and implementing workplace plans. Take the trouble to *really* understand the fee structure—fees for the advisor, the investment provider, and the investments themselves—as those costs have a direct and potentially enormous impact on your investment outcome, and therefore ultimately your retirement income. Require the plan to include "index fund" investment choices for potentially better performance for you and your employees (see "Invest Efficiently" section of this chapter for an explanation).

If you're a sole proprietor, don't assume you can't create a 401(k) plan for yourself—you certainly can, but again, the administrative requirements may mean extra work, or outsourcing to a third party. The tax advantages and growth potential may be worthwhile if you're going to contribute enough to offset costs when compared to non-tax-advantaged options.

If you're not in a position to launch a tax-advantaged workplace retirement plan for your own savings (and as an employee retention tool), consider opening a traditional IRA and/or Roth IRA. If you want to contribute more than the IRS allows, open a separate non-tax-advantaged ("non-qualified") account and look for Federal and/or State tax-free investments choices to help manage the tax burden. Your working spouse can open a separate IRA as well, up to IRS limits.

5.

Tax Management

Somewhere, right now, someone in Congress may be dreaming up a clever new way to separate you from your money. Get a tax advisor who aims to be just as clever.
-John Piatchek

IMPORTANT: We are not accountants or tax professionals so this chapter should be taken as general information, not tax advice specific to your situation.

BOTTOM LINE: Educate yourself and work with professionals to help you avoid giving the U.S. Treasury more than legally required.

Tax preparation computer software may work well for some filers, but make sure you're using a reputable provider and a version that is updated when tax rules change, and make sure the software provider stands behind the results with enforceable guarantees.

Seek both tax credits and tax deductions...there are many, and they may change frequently, so review options with a professional.

Take advantage of all legally permissible opportunities to defer taxes, or avoid taxes entirely, on special IRS items related to health care, college funding, business expenses, child care, and potentially other expenses.

Understand the basics of Social Security taxation if you are in or near retirement, and how various types of income in retirement (both earned income and investment income) may affect your Social Security benefits and taxes.

Landlords, investors with "passive" income, business owners, and self-employed individuals are subject to special IRS rules; high-income earners may be subject to Alternative Minimum Tax (AMT) rules. Proceed carefully with professional guidance to take advantage of tax relief opportunities within the tax code.

Be aware of special tax provisions if you have a trust or are considering creating one (with the assistance of a legal professional).

Understand the "Kiddie Tax" if you have minor children with unearned (investment) income.

Comply with IRS document retention guidelines in case of an audit. Refer to other sections of this book for further general tax information, but (and we can't say this too often) it is always important to work closely with a qualified tax professional.

THE TEAM

Almost everyone needs sooner or later:

Financial Planning Professional
Investment professional (some CFP®, ChFC or other financial planning professionals are qualified for this role).
Accountant

And for some:
Attorney
Business accountant or business tax specialist

DO-SOME-OF-IT-YOURSELFERS: If your situation is simple enough you may be able to prepare your own taxes, especially with readily available software which does a pretty good job of walking you through the steps. *But if you have any doubt about your ability to manage this critical piece of your financial puzzle, get professional assistance.*

⌐⌐⌐⌐⌐⌐⌐⌐⌐⌐⌐⌐⌐⌐⌐⌐⌐⌐⌐⌐⌐⌐⌐⌐⌐⌐

How it works in the real world: We're not accountants or attorneys, so we don't give specific tax or legal advice—we work with your team on those—but we can speak in general terms about tax and legal concepts.

Not long ago a new client asked for guidance relating to some grazing land he owned, part of which he wanted to sell to one of the farmers who was leasing it. He was facing a considerable capital gains tax bill due to the increase in value since he inherited it many decades ago. He had income of around $50,000 per year from other sources and wanted to know if we had any ideas.

We directed him to his accountant for the final word, but we told him that the long-term capital gains tax rate that year for married filers was zero percent if their adjusted gross income (AGI) was less than $79,500. So if their AGI was say $38,000, they would have a $41,500 cushion before they owed capital gains tax.

They could sell part of the land this year, keeping gains just under the AGI threshold, then re-evaluate next year and sell some more.

Again, their accountant would need to be involved, which is why we love the team approach to planning, but our new client felt a little better now.

Don't assume there are no solutions to financial issues that may appear to be insurmountable—talk to your advisory team.

∟∟∟∟∟∟∟∟∟∟∟∟∟∟∟∟∟∟∟∟∟∟∟∟∟∟∟∟

You have the potential to dramatically ease your tax burden by taking advantage of a variety of techniques, from contributing to your tax-deferred workplace retirement plan, to using tax-free cash value life insurance policies to build emergency cash, to including Federal tax-free municipal bonds in your taxable investments. The better you understand your tax situation, the better your results may be, so take the trouble to study this topic and ask questions of your tax professional. IRS.gov has also become a decent resource in recent years—easier to navigate than it used to be, and generally written in easy-to-understand language.

Let's Not Repeat Ourselves Too Much…

Throughout this book we have provided guidance on tax advantages and pitfalls in the context of particular financial planning situations. Please refer to these chapter sections to review those ideas:

Income, Budget, And Accumulation Planning
- "Budget Planning: Basic Living Expenses"
- "Debt Free By Choice: Sweating The Small Stuff"
- "Earmark Windfalls"
- "College Savings Accumulation"

Risk Management
- "Risk Management Critical Zone II: Health Care"
- "Health Savings Account: Quadruple Tax Play"
- "Health Savings Account: IRA Supercharger For Age 65+"
- "Health Care Outside The Box"
- "Take Some Healthy Tax Breaks"
- "Medicare" (Medicare Medical Savings Account)
- "Permanent Life Insurance: 'Owning Protection,' And A Roth-Like Feature"
- "Taxation Of Life Insurance"
- "The Life Insurance Triangle Of Doom"
- "A Life Insurance Strategy For 'Lazy' Or 'Crazy' Money"
- "Risk Management Critical Zone IV: Disability Insurance"

Investing
- "Invest Efficiently"
- "Investment Tax Efficiency: 401(k)'s, 403(b)'s, IRA's…And 'Non-Qualified' Investments'"
- "Capital Gains Are Great! Capital Gains Tax, Not So Much"
- "When Is Selling Low A Good Thing?"
- "Annuities"
- "Income-Producing Investments (And Their Tax Consequences)"
- "Rental Real Estate: You're The Landlord!"
- "Do-It-Yourself Investor Dangers"

Tax Management
- o All of it!

Estate Planning
- o "The Estate Tax Exclusion Pendulum"
- o "Intra-Family Gifting"
- o "Life Insurance As A Source Of Estate Liquidity"
- o "*Nothing* Should Go Through Probate!" (okay not a tax, but a government-imposed fee you can easily avoid)
- o "Wills And Trusts (Dump Truck Or Courier Service?)"
- o "The Power Of Stepped-Up Basis"
- o "IRA Beneficiaries (Including Tax Considerations)"

Retirement
- o "Retirement Accumulation Planning"
- o "'Big 10' Retirement Planning Components" (#6)
- o "Don't Jump The Gun On Drawing From Tax Deferred Accounts!"
- o "The Mother Of All Tax Penalties: Missing Your RMD's"
- o "Retirement, Succession, And Contingency Planning For Business Owners"

rrrrrrrrrrrrrrrrrrrrrrrrr

The Ultimate Tax Break: Tax Credits

A tax credit is better than a tax deduction which only reduces the amount of income on which you owe tax. A tax credit directly reduces the total amount of tax you owe on a dollar for dollar basis.

For example if you receive a $1,000 tax credit for child care, you will owe the IRS $1,000 less than you would have owed without the credit.

Here are a few tax credits available at the time of this writing (seek professional guidance for current rules):

- **The Earned Income Tax Credit**: if you make less than a certain amount of money in your employment, the IRS may reward you for your effort with a tax credit—potentially resulting in a refund even if you didn't owe tax to begin with.

- **College-related tax credits:** There are programs available to assist individuals and families with college tuition and other expenses…each has different rules so it's important to choose the right one. Seek advice from an experienced tax professional or university financial aid department.

- **Child And Dependent Care Tax Credit:** If you pay for babysitting or day care so you can work, you may qualify for assistance in the form of tax credits. Under certain circumstances this credit can also help offset expenses for the care of a disabled spouse or dependent who can't care for themselves.

- **"Savers" tax credit:** If you earn less than a certain level of income, you may be able to receive a tax credit simply for participating in your employer's retirement savings plan. This is on *top* of the tax deferral you'll enjoy on the money you contribute to the retirement plan—essentially putting money back into your pocket as a reward for saving.

- **Adoption credit:** This credit can help cover expenses for adoption fees, attorney and court costs, even travel expenses for the adoption of a child who qualifies under IRS rules.

- **Special short term tax credit offers:** "Clean energy" cars and appliances, energy-saving heating and air conditioning systems, even expenses for materials to seal existing home windows can potentially save you money on your utility bills or other energy-related expenses—and may make your local power plant have to work just a little less, so local, State, and Federal governments may offer tax credits periodically to encourage these purchases.

- **Other tax credits:** The range of tax credit opportunities changes frequently, so check IRS.gov yearly, and work with a qualified tax professional (have we ever mentioned that?).

The Next Best Thing To A Tax Credit: Tax Deduction

While a tax credit directly reduces the tax you owe on a dollar for dollar basis, a tax deduction only reduces the *income* on which you owe tax. So you save the amount of tax you would have owed on that dollar amount...for example if your effective tax rate is 25% and you give $1,000 to a qualified charity, you won't have to pay the $250 of tax that you would normally have paid on that $1,000.

Here are examples of deductions available as of this writing:

- Charitable donations
- Certain interest expenses including home mortgage
- Professional fees
- Moving expenses related to employment
- Child care expenses
- Union dues
- Safe deposit box fees
- Tax preparation fees
- Business expenses if you're self-employed, potentially including depreciation of buildings and equipment used in your self-employment...perhaps even your home office if it meets very specific criteria
- Investment costs...including, believe it or not, magazine subscriptions you purchase for investing advice (but you may not be surprised that we encourage you to engage with a professional investment advisor instead!)

- "Bad debt" deduction (you loaned money and they didn't pay you back—specific rules apply)

There may be many other deductions available for your particular situation, so make sure you're getting current information and working with—you guessed it—a qualified tax professional.

Charitable Tax Deductions

Giving to qualified charities (non-profits) can lower your tax bill, potentially offsetting up to 50% of your Adjusted Gross Income (AGI) for tax purposes.

The amount of offset may depend on the type of organization to whom you donate, so get professional guidance—for example, you may be able to deduct property that has appreciated, which is a great tax management opportunity, but you may only be able to deduct up 30% of your AGI for that; and you may be able to "carry over" deductions for excess charitable donations to future years. But as always, work with a tax professional to make sure you're operating within current regulations.

Be sure your charitable giving is to a "qualified organization" per IRS rules (see irs.gov and your tax professional for guidance). And if you receive anything of value in return for your contribution, such as goods or "free" advertising for example, you may only deduct the difference in value.

The donation of a vehicle falls under special IRS rules, so get professional advice before proceeding.

There are online resources for valuing donations of non-cash contributions such as clothing, electronics, tools, furniture, and household items, which the IRS will generally accept in an audit.

However if you give cash *or* non-cash items worth more than a certain amount ($250 as of this writing), you must meet other documentation requirements for the IRS, so get professional guidance. The IRS website irs.gov has more information on this topic.

Keep good records of tax deductible donations, such as cancelled checks (business owners see below).

Accelerated Deductions

If your tax professional projects next year's tax bill to be higher or lower than the current year, you may wish to adjust the timing of deductible activities to even out the tax burden.

For example let's say you're planning to give $5,000 to a charity each year, totaling $10,000 across this year and next year. If your income tax is going to be more for the current year than you expect it to be next year, you could give more to the charity this year (an "accelerated deduction") to potentially reduce your total tax burden over those two years.

You may be able to similarly accelerate deductions for professional fees and dues (even magazine subscriptions) required for your self-employment business; replacing outdated business equipment; securities loss sales; and other items. Work closely with a business tax professional.

The Power Of Tax Deferral And Tax-Free Spending

We've advocated for deferring taxes throughout this book, but let's think this through once again.

If you had one dollar and doubled it every year, and paid no taxes, how much would you have in twenty years?

$1,048,576.

If instead you paid 25% tax on that first dollar, doubled the remaining $.75, paid 25% tax on that growth, and continued that way every year for twenty years, how much would you have?

$95,249.

This is an extreme example because you can't double your money every year (right?), but it illustrates the power of tax deferral.

How about a more realistic example: let's start with $100,000, and instead of doubling every year, add 8% growth per year with no taxes: in twenty years you'd have $503,383.

With 25% taxes on the growth each year you'd have $339,956...32% less money.

So take full advantage of workplace retirement savings plans, and/or individually owned IRA's, to defer taxation as long as possible.

And take advantage of every opportunity to pay for items with tax-free money (Federal and State tax-free): Health Savings Accounts, Flexible Spending Accounts for healthcare expenses, and Flexible Spending Accounts for child care allow you to set aside money out of your paychecks before taxes, and you *never* pay tax on that money as long as you use it for allowable expenses. We talk more about some of these techniques elsewhere in this chapter.

Social Security Taxation

When FDR signed Social Security into law, he promised Social Security would never be taxed.

It's generally a bad idea to make promises about the future, especially on behalf of Congress. This one didn't pan out.

Social Security is still not taxed up to a certain earnings level, which Congress can adjust—you should look up the current number right now if you don't know the threshold for your situation (married or single). Work with your accountant or tax preparer to plan for the hit you may take at tax time.

Whether you pay tax on Social Security, and how much, depends largely on the amount of income you bring in from other sources such as:

- Self-employment including real estate income (rental properties for example)
- Stock dividends
- Bond or other interest including tax-free income from municipal bonds
- Taxable pension payments
- Taxable withdrawals from 401(k) and Traditional IRA accounts
- Other items which must be reported on your tax return

Understand how these income sources drive your Social Security into the taxable range, and strategically reduce them if possible on a year-by-year basis.

For example withdrawing tax-free funds from your Roth IRA instead of your tax-deferred traditional IRA if you're close to the income threshold could potentially keep you from being taxed on your Social Security (or keep you from being taxed as much).

Self-Employment Tax

Being your own boss can be great, but it's an entire tax world unto itself. This is important enough to repeat: work with an experienced, knowledgeable business accountant, and a similarly qualified attorney, to help you avoid pitfalls and find ways to potentially reduce your tax burden.

For example, as with personal taxes don't miss opportunities to take business tax deductions. Below are a few examples—but again, we can't stress enough that IRS rules change over time, so you must work with an experienced tax professional and/or up-to-date software to get these right. **And document everything carefully...receipts, utility bills, everything should be kept on file for required timeframes:**

- Business use of home or dwelling (home office)...can even include the portion of your utility bill applicable to that room or rooms, *but firm IRS rules apply*

- Automobile expenses and other modes of travel—airfare, bus fare, etc.

- Educational expenses including books, lab fees etc.—even webinars and e-books may be deductible if purchased to improve your business

- Depreciation of property and equipment

- Banking fees

- Advertising expenses

- Health insurance premiums (may result in a tax credit instead of a tax deduction—even better)

- Restaurant meals and entertainment expenses, *if necessary to the business*

If you're self-employed, take all available deductions, and also look for ways to reduce your taxable income to start with. Here are a few examples (work with a tax professional to make sure these are still available):

- Create a defined benefit pension plan or age-weighted profit-sharing plan for yourself; besides helping you save for retirement, these types of plans can help reduce taxable income.

- If you own your own building for business purposes (under an IRS-recognized business entity structure such as an LLC), you may be able to pay yourself rent and deduct the expense, thus reducing your gross taxable income.

- If you're a self-employed professional and are required to maintain liability insurance, you may be able to set up your own insurance company specifically for your business, which may save costs and still allow a tax deduction for the premiums. This is tricky and should be guided by an experienced business accountant or attorney.

Finally, if you are required to pay estimated tax, make sure you do so within deadlines to avoid penalties.

A Word To All Business Owners

You generally must take deductions for charitable donations on your individual tax return, *not* on your business taxes, even if the donation was made under the business name. There are limited exceptions so work closely with a tax professional. You must itemize deductions on your tax return in order to claim charitable deductions—and as for documentation: *for a donation made under a business name, a cancelled check may **not** be sufficient—for an IRS audit you must have an acknowledgement letter from the non-profit.*

Alternative Minimum Tax (AMT) Tips

The Alternative Minimum Tax (AMT) was designed to prevent wealthy taxpayers from benefiting "too much" from tax exemptions and deductions. But because many of the thresholds that trigger the AMT are not indexed to automatically increase with rising incomes, more people are subject to the AMT now than when it was enacted.

Your tax professional can help determine if you're able to take all available deductions…or whether instead you may be subject to the AMT formula.

There's no legal way around the AMT, but there are a few money management alternatives which can help reduce your burden:

- **Use your employer's flexible spending benefit:** If you buy your own medical insurance on the individual market, you can only tax-deduct medical expenses if they are more than a certain percentage of your adjusted gross income (AGI) but this restriction does not apply if you participate in a qualified workplace "flexible spending" plan. This reduces your taxable income under both regular tax calculations and the AMT.

- **Encourage your employer to use an "accountable" expense plan:** If you don't have to turn in receipts to your employer for expenses related to your job, but instead deduct some or all of those expenses on your personal tax return, you may lose those deductions under the AMT. If instead your employer reimburses you directly for expenses, it's not counted as part of your income tax picture (at least not as of this writing).

- **Incentive stock options (ISO's):** These may trigger the AMT; work with your accountant or tax planner to seek ways to potentially reduce your burden, including timing of exercising the options and/or selling stocks obtained through such programs.

- **Depreciation of rental property and/or other business assets (post-1986):** You may benefit from a longer period of "stretching" depreciation; work closely with your tax professional.

- **Keep looking for new twists:** The above are just a few suggestions; there may be other valuable techniques for reducing your AMT burden, and Congress occasionally alters AMT rules, so make sure your accountant or tax preparer (or tax preparation software) is up to date.

Trust Tax

As of this writing, if you create a trust under your Social Security number, the activity in the trust (income, capital gains, etc.) is treated as your own activity for tax purposes.

However if the trust has its own tax ID, the trust receives very different, *generally less favorable*, tax treatment. So if you don't need to give a trust its own tax ID for some specific reason, then it may make sense not to do so. Work closely with your attorney and tax professional to determine the right course of action.

If trust income (from stock dividends or bond interest for example) is distributed to beneficiaries, the trust may receive a tax deduction, and beneficiaries may be taxed on the income.

If instead the income is retained by the trust, the trust may owe the income tax…and if the trust is under your Social Security number, that may mean *you* owe the tax. Work with your tax professional to make sure you know the current tax rules for your state, and to determine whether (and how much) income could be managed differently for better tax efficiency.

Of course state taxes may also apply to your trust; if your state has a high tax rate, you may be able to transfer assets to a trust you create in a different state with a lower tax burden. Seek professional state-specific tax and legal advice.

Finally, trust administrative expenses above a certain percentage "floor" may be tax deductible. Make sure your tax professional is knowledgeable and experienced with trusts so you don't miss any of these potentially valuable tax provisions.

Kiddie Tax

A formerly-popular tax management technique was to transfer "unearned" (investment) income to children to enjoy a lower tax bracket. Congress stopped most of this by enacting "kiddie tax" rules requiring such income beyond a certain threshold to be taxed at the parents' rate.

However this applies to *income* from investments, not growth (capital gains)...so for example if you give your child stocks which then grow in value but generate little or no income, you may be more likely to stay within the maximum limits before being subject to the kiddie tax.

Once your child is beyond a certain age, they will no longer be subject to the kiddie tax. Work closely with your tax professional to make sure you comply with the law while taking advantage of provisions which may reduce your taxes.

Passive Activity And At-Risk Rules For Investors And Landlords

We all love tax deductions, but for landlords and investors—who receive what the IRS considers "passive income"—deducting business expenses can be a minefield.

Normally if you own (or co-own) a business, you can deduct all kinds of expenses to reduce your tax burden—deductions for equipment, overhead, services, repairs, furniture, fixtures, depreciation of the building, and many other items.

However if you fall under the definition of a "passive owner" because you do not actually work a certain number of hours per year in the business for example (and that number may be subject to change by the IRS, so work with your tax professional to make sure you're getting current information), then you may not be able to use some (or any) of those deductions.

As of this writing, if you're a landlord *but not a licensed real estate professional,* your activities are considered passive regardless of how much work you put into your rentals.

That's not to say you can't take any tax deductions at all…you may be able to deduct advertising costs, depreciation, management fees, cleaning and maintenance, supplies—even pest control and other items. But there are special limits when compared to deductions for real estate professionals, and rules can change, so **work closely with a tax professional to understand current IRS requirements.**

The IRS does allow deductions for repairs to rental property, but take special note of the difference between a "repair" and an "improvement." If you upgrade the kitchen or add insulation, those are considered improvements. You can't deduct those, but you can depreciate them over several years using IRS tables, thus potentially reducing your long-term tax burden.

If you live in a property yourself part of the year and also rent it out part of the year, you may be able to take some deductions and claim some losses against your tax burden, but again, the rules are complicated, so work with an experienced professional.

The IRS also prohibits offsetting your passive gains (or losses) with non-passive gains (or losses). For example as of this writing you can't offset income from employment with losses from your rentals or other passive activities.

How Long Should You Keep Tax Records?

According to the IRS as of this writing, you should keep tax forms, relevant receipts for charitable donations, and other deductible items, etc. until three years from the date you filed the original return, or two years from the date you paid the tax (whichever is later).

The timeframe is seven years if you claim a loss from worthless securities (e.g. you bought an individual company stock like WorldCom and the stock went to zero value—like WorldCom!); there is also a seven-year document retention requirement for a "bad debt" deduction (you loaned money and they didn't pay you back…this is a special tax situation—work closely with your tax preparer or accountant on this and all other special circumstances).

IRA Beneficiaries (Including Tax Considerations): see Estate Planning chapter.

Tax Treatment Of Investments: see Investing chapter.

6.

Estate Planning

A client wanted to make sure his business would pass to his son when he died, make sure debts were paid, and provide for his wife's financial security. Now whenever the son sees me in public he always gives me a big hug and introduces me as "the guy who saved his business." I can't imagine a more humbling and gratifying endorsement.

-John Piatchek

IMPORTANT: We are not attorneys so this chapter should be taken as general information, not legal advice specific to your situation.

***BOTTOM LINE:** Get current tax and legal advice from a professional for your own situation in relation to the general concepts we discuss in this chapter. Estate planning rules may have changed since publication of this book.*

Estate planning is about passing your assets to others by gift during life, and/or by bequest at death, as efficiently as possible, so that the recipients receive more of what you intend to give them, and other entities such as the IRS and probate courts receive as little as legally allowable.

Take care of your estate planning now: when it's too late, it's too late!

If your estate is larger than the current gift tax and estate tax exclusion amounts, work with your accountant and attorney on estate planning techniques which may help reduce your burden (but which are beyond the scope of this book).

Life insurance may be an efficient way to provide heirs with the necessary funds to pay estate tax on their inheritance, if the size of your estate exceeds the estate tax exclusion amount at your death. Work with legal and/or tax professionals to weigh pros and cons of gifting assets during your lifetime, versus leaving bequests for heirs after your death.

Avoid potentially significant probate costs for your heirs by specifying a beneficiary for each of your assets which has an account number, title, or deed, or is of significant value. A will does not avoid probate, and therefore becomes a public document; a trust does avoid probate, and remains private.

Married couples in many states (including our state of Missouri) can potentially protect assets from creditors by titling joint accounts "Tenants By The Entirety," instead of the commonly-used "Joint Tenants With Rights Of Survivorship." Get legal guidance regarding laws in your own state.

Everyone should have: a will; a Power Of Attorney document naming someone to handle your financial affairs in case of your incapacity; a Medical Power Of Attorney specifying someone to make health care decisions on your behalf in case of incapacity;

and a Medical Directive ("Living Will") to specify certain health care wishes in case of incapacity. Get professional legal assistance.

A will may specify a guardian for minor children, and distributes assets within a short time after your death to your specified heirs.

A trust can carry out more complicated distribution instructions which you specify—and over a longer (though not unlimited) period of time. Seek legal guidance.

A trust may be "irrevocable," allowing you to transfer ownership—and control—of your assets to the trust during your lifetime; this may be desirable to shelter assets from inclusion in your estate for estate tax purposes; limit access for a special-needs beneficiary for Medicaid qualification purposes; and other reasons. Trust rules vary by state, so seek qualified and experienced legal guidance.

Assets which pass to heirs at your death receive "stepped-up basis"—a "reset" of value for capital gains tax purposes. This may be preferable to gifting a highly appreciated asset during your lifetime, which could be subject to tax on those gains. Work with your tax professional to understand current rules.

Understand the tax ramifications of various beneficiary scenarios for your IRA and other tax-advantaged accounts.

Business owners: review "Risk Management For Business Owners" in the Risk Management chapter for "death of owner" planning concepts; discuss estate planning ramifications of your business entity type with experienced tax and legal professionals; and anywhere we refer to "assets" in this chapter, also think "my company."

Once again: your financial advisor (and this book) may speak in general informational terms about important legal and tax matters, but you must engage licensed and experienced attorneys and accountants to get specific advice—and documents—to address *your own situation.*

THE TEAM
Almost everyone needs sooner or later:
    Financial planning professional
    Investment professional for account titling and beneficiary strategies (some but not all CFP®, ChFC or other financial planning professionals are qualified for this role).
    Accountant (and for some: a business accountant)
    Attorney (and for some: a business estate planning specialist)
    Life insurance professional
    Real estate agent or broker
    Long-term care insurance professional

DO-SOME-OF-IT-YOURSELFERS: You can do a lot more estate planning yourself than you might realize. Titling your assets correctly to avoid probate is not difficult for the most part (except for the beneficiary deed on your home which may require the assistance of a professional).

But avoid do-it-yourself wills and trusts, and other critical estate planning documents…it's absolutely worth the cost of an attorney to get those right for your sake, and for the sake of your loved ones. Similarly, tax planning in the context of your estate and gift planning activities should be coordinated with a professional tax advisor.

┌─┌─┌─┌─┌─┌─┌─┌─┌─┌─┌─┌─┌─┌─┌─┌─┌─┌─┌─

How it works in the real world: One of our favorite couples, Mr. and Mrs. W—successful local farmers, world travelers, big believers in community service, and with a sense of humor to boot—had their adult children working on their farm. In fact the kids had a lot of "sweat equity" in the family business, enough to earn an ownership stake.

One of Mr. and Mrs. W's sons is ready to carry on the tradition—in fact *loves* farming—but the other son is a talented and hard-working budding artist...who is ready to make his way in the art world and leave farming behind. He understands he won't receive his ownership stake until the family farm is sold someday.

The W's were worried about whether, or how, their boys would be able to work things out if Mr. and Mrs. W were to die prematurely, without having to potentially destroy the farm with a partial sale, or some other unattractive option, to provide the artist son his share.

After talking through various ideas with their advisors, Mr. and Mrs. W decided to leave the farm to the farmer son in a few years, and as a contingency, they purchased a "second to die" life insurance policy with the artist son as beneficiary—with the death benefit of the life insurance equal to the value of the farm at the time the artist son left for the big city. So if both Mr. and Mrs. W passed, the artist son would be made whole and relinquish his 50% ownership of the farm to the farmer son.

Mr. and Mrs. W likely would not have come up with this creative estate planning solution without the help of their team of advisors—their attorney, accountant, financial advisor, and life insurance professional. Don't be shy about sharing your concerns and dreams with your advisors...and let them know when it appears your financial life could be headed for a left turn, even if you can't see right now how they might help.

The Estate Tax Exclusion Pendulum

Since it was implemented in 1916, the estate tax, also known as the "death tax," has evolved in a number of ways. The lifetime limit on how much money you could gift to others or leave to heirs without being subject to the estate tax—known as the "estate tax exclusion"—has been as low as $50,000 in some periods, and is well over $5 million as of this writing. Be sure to keep up on current rules by talking to your tax accountant and/or financial advisor.

When the exclusion number is lower, many more people face the problem of burdening heirs with a terrible dilemma: sacrificing to government coffers a significant portion of hard-earned assets which their deceased loved one generously bequeathed to them.

Whoever inherits your assets must pay the estate tax to the government within a specified period of time (nine months as of this writing). If the assets are not easy to sell, for example real estate, a house, or other illiquid holdings, your heirs may have to come up with the money by liquidating taxable accounts—resulting in even more taxes—selling other more liquid holdings, or paying out of their own pocket.

Each person in the U.S. is entitled to their own estate and gift tax exclusions, so each member of a married couple has their own separate exclusion. As of this writing one spouse can leave everything to the other spouse with no estate tax consequence—the "marital deduction"—but after the death of the second spouse, there will only be one exemption allowed.

For many situations, a better arrangement may be to set up a marital trust to shelter part of the assets. Seek professional guidance from an estate planning attorney for any such strategy.

During periods when the exclusion is a high enough number, the estate tax may not be an issue for many of us. That's great...enjoy it while it lasts, and who knows, it may last a very long time. But the underlying justifications for estate taxation can be back on the table at any time in Congress, and the exclusion could be lowered once again.

Sensible financial planning should include a discussion with your financial advisor and your accountant about the ramifications for you if and when the exclusion drops again.

Intra-Family Gifting

Before 1976 taxpayers would commonly give away their assets to family members in order to avoid estate tax when they died. The IRS soon caught on, and Congress combined many of the rules for estate tax and gift tax to eliminate this loophole. There are still important differences in the details, so work with tax and legal professionals.

Any and all gifts are subject to the gift tax. A "gift" is anything you give freely out of affection or to help someone, without receiving similar value in return. The gift *giver* is subject to the gift tax.

Fortunately there is an exclusion for the gift tax—so you (and your spouse separately) can give up that amount each year without having to pay gift tax. And you can give to as many different individuals as you wish, with the exclusion figured separately for each separate gift-receiver. The exclusion amount changes periodically so be sure you and your tax professional have up-to-date information.

If you plan to leave substantial assets to your family when you die, consider gifts during your lifetime as well. One advantage is that you'll be around to see the looks on their faces! Another benefit is that you can maximize the gifts up to your annual gift exclusion amount in order to help hedge against the possibility that the estate tax exclusion may change in an unfavorable direction in the future. However assets which are highly appreciated and not tax deferred, such as non-IRA stocks or real estate which have grown in value, or which you expect will grow in value, will receive a stepped-up basis for your heirs at your death under current IRS rules (see "The Power Of Stepped-Up Basis" section later in this chapter)—so consider *not* passing those along during your lifetime. Also remember that Medicaid has a five year look-back for purposes of long term care assistance at the time of publication of this book, so any assets you gifted within five years before seeking long term care services will be considered by Medicaid in their evaluation.

Whether or not you believe your assets will be subject to the estate or gift tax, you should have a basic understanding of rules around giving gifts to family members. Helping a child or grandchild with their expenses so they can fully fund their 401(k) or Roth IRA or other tax deferred retirement savings vehicle, or gifts to their College 529 or other tax-advantaged account for higher education expenses, are great ways to show your love *and* manage taxes for both yourself and the next generation (or the next two—*but seek professional advice regarding transfers to grandchildren, as "generation-skipping transfers" carry their own set of tax rules with heavy penalties for noncompliance*).

Life Insurance As A Source Of Estate Liquidity

If you die with enough assets to be subject to the estate tax, your heirs will have to figure out how to fulfill that obligation.

Selling some of those assets (in time to meet IRS deadlines) is one option; taking out a loan is another…but for many clients, the simplest and most cost effective solution may be life insurance earmarked to cover the estate tax bill. This has been a well-used financial planning technique for decades.

If you purchased permanent life insurance as part of your estate planning and watched the tax code pendulum swing in your favor, think carefully before allowing that policy to lapse. Review your total life insurance needs with your advisor to make sure there aren't other important reasons to keep the coverage— supplemental retirement funding (using cash value in the policy), family protection, eliminating a home mortgage or other debt in case of your death, income replacement, final expenses, and other one-time or recurring expenses your survivors may face.

You may even wish to keep the policy in force and leave the proceeds to your favorite charity—a gift that can keep on giving long after you're gone.

Keep the policy if it serves some purpose, drop it if not...but again, think carefully as there's no way to predict how estate tax laws may change, and the "pennies for dollars" nature of life insurance is unique—and more difficult to reconstruct the older you get.

Nothing Should Go Through Probate!

Nothing you pass to your heirs should cause them to have to pay a court to review and validate your will (or worse yet, pay the court to decide where everything goes if you have *no* will). That's what probate is— a judge verifying the validity of your will, resolving disputes or problems with the will, determining heirs in the absence of a will, and other associated activities.

The cost to your heirs for this "service" varies from state to state, so ask your advisor about your own state; and if your estate is small enough, probate may not be required at all (the value threshold varies by state as well).

But in many states the cost to heirs is in the 5-10% range, so if you leave a $200,000 house to your kids, and probate costs 6%, that's $12,000 the kids have to pay within a specified timeframe before they really own the house. How will they come up with that, without having to sell the house?

The better question is, why *should* they have to come up with it at all?

Avoiding probate for your heirs is simple: just make sure you specify beneficiaries for everything you own which has an account number, title, or deed, or is of significant value.

- **Anything with an account number:** bank accounts, investment accounts, etc.: for a bank account simply talk to a bank teller; for any other types of account talk to customer service at the company which holds the account, and simply tell them you want to add beneficiaries. They will provide a form for you to complete and sign. That's it. No probate.

- **Anything with a title:** cars, boats, trailers, etc.: same idea, just visit your local vehicle licensing office, tell them you want beneficiaries, and they'll produce a form for you to sign. That's it. No probate.

- **Anything with a deed:** real estate: this is a bit more complicated…generally this documentation has to be registered at a courthouse, so get assistance from a title company or attorney. If you're getting a will or other documents with an attorney anyway, deed registration may be part of a package deal. That's it. No probate.

- **Anything of significant value which doesn't have an account number, title, or deed:** a business; jewelry; art, guitars, guns, antiques, or other collectibles: if you own it, can describe it clearly in writing, and it's transferrable, a properly written and notarized document can be executed (sometimes called a "beneficiary bill of sale" or "beneficiary transfer instrument"). That's it. No probate.

Smaller personal items won't require probate unless there is a dispute about who should receive items.

Make sure beneficiaries know where assets are located (and the deeds or other supporting documentation)…so they can avoid confusion and conflict, in addition to avoiding probate. And if you use a bank safe deposit box, be sure you designate a beneficiary for it as well!

Special Titling For Special Married Couples

Ok, *all* married couples are special. But some states (exactly half as of this writing, including our home state of Missouri) make you extra-special by allowing a unique type of joint titling of assets called "Tenants By The Entirety." This can provide significant protection against creditors (but always seek professional legal advice for your particular situation).

In the past, joint bank accounts, investments, real estate deeds, etc. were often titled "Joint Tenants With Rights Of Survivorship" or "JTWROS." In fact if you look at your investment statements and bank statements right now (and you should), you may still see this outdated and potentially dangerous form of joint titling, as we commonly see when analyzing accounts for new clients. With this form of joint ownership, if one of the two owners happens to owe money to a creditor, the creditor may be able to put a lien on the account.

For example if a husband is found liable in a wrongful death auto accident lawsuit, the winner of the lawsuit can go after the husband's half of that account.

But with special "Tenants By The Entirety" titling, the husband is seen by the courts as owning 100% of the account…and *simultaneously* the wife is *also* seen as owning 100% of the account.

So now the creditor in the wrongful death lawsuit example could *not* touch the account, because the wife legally owns 100% of it…and the creditor has no claim against her.

If you are a married couple in a state that allows Tenants By The Entirety titling but still have assets with the old JTWROS titling, call your advisor right away (or the company, bank, etc. who holds the account), and tell them you want to correct this oversight. It only requires a simple form and may save you a lot of grief. If in doubt, seek professional legal advice for your particular situation before taking action.

Powers Of Attorney

A **"Durable Power Of Attorney For Finances"** is a legal document authorizing a particular person to act on your behalf in financial matters if you become incapacitated.

- This document gives the person of your choice the ability to cash your checks, pay your bills, or sell your home—in other words, any and all financial decisions and actions they believe you would wish to have happen if you were not incapacitated.

- Without a legally executed durable power of attorney document, you would need a court order even to cash your spouse's Social Security check.

- Many attorneys include this document as part of an estate planning package, in addition to drafting your will and/or trust for example.

- Take care of this important directive *now* while you're still able. When it's too late, it's too late!

- Be sure to have a discussion with the person you're choosing for this solemn duty; let them know your general philosophy and wishes for how you want your finances handled, but ultimately they need to understand that they will be responsible for using their best judgment on your behalf.

A **"Durable Power Of Attorney For Health Care Decisions"** provides legal authorization for a particular person to make decisions on your behalf regarding your medical care, if you are unable to do so yourself. Have this document notarized, and let your loved ones (and of course the person you designate to make the decisions) know where it is located, as the hospital or other medical care providers will need to see the original document. Hospitals may be able to provide a do-it-yourself form for this document, but we recommend a review by your attorney to be sure it's correctly written.

An **"Advance Healthcare Directive"** or **"Living Will"** is a document that spells out the kind of medical care you want if you become medically incapacitated, and where the outlook is not good. For example would you want a feeding tube, cardiopulmonary resuscitation, or other specific extraordinary measures to prolong your life if there was little or no chance of recovery? The person you have designated under your power of attorney for health care decisions, as well as medical caregivers, will attempt to honor your wishes to the best of their ability. Of course you can't think of every contingency, so there is always the possibility of a "best judgment" situation, but spelling out your wishes for common medical circumstances can help provide a sense of your general wishes. This document should be notarized and kept in a safe place. And your loved ones should be aware of your wishes so there is less chance of conflict if and when your directives need to be carried out.

Review on a regular basis your durable power of attorney, power of attorney for healthcare decisions, and advance healthcare directive, and make changes when needed.

There are other types of powers of attorney beyond the scope of this book; seek professional legal guidance if you need someone to act on your behalf in important matters, either temporarily (for example if you're going to be out of the country) or permanently.

Wills And Trusts (Dump Truck Or Courier Service?)

A **will** provides instructions for distribution of your assets at death (including a "pour over" provision if you also have a trust—in case you forgot to title any assets in the name of the trust).

A will can also designate a guardian for your minor or disabled dependents.

A will is like a dump truck—assets are generally distributed within a limited time after your death to the people or entities named in the will. Although it's possible to include more complicated provisions in a will, a trust may be better suited to stretch distributions over time or in other complex ways (and a trust avoids probate).

Here are other considerations regarding wills:

- **A will does *not* avoid probate**—in fact one common purpose of probate court is to certify the legitimacy of a will. Probate is a public proceeding and becomes part of the public record, so if privacy is important to you, consider a trust in addition to your will (or correct titling of your assets—see "*Nothing* Should Go Through Probate" section). **Seek professional legal guidance.**

- If you have a trust, the provisions of the trust for distributing assets to your beneficiaries will **override your will**, as long as the assets are titled in the name of the trust. Otherwise, your will may have "pour over" provisions to move overlooked assets into the trust...but only after going through probate first. Get in the habit of designating your trust as the owner of newly-acquired assets every time.

- If you have named beneficiaries on assets with account numbers, titles, or deeds, and any other assets of significant value, those beneficiary designations will override both your will and your trust, and will also avoid probate (again see "*Nothing* Should Go Through Probate" section for more details).

- You must name an executor in the will—a person you trust to carry out the provisions of the will. This person also handles other administrative necessities such as creating an inventory of your assets, notifying investment advisors and/or investment companies, retirement plan administrators, etc.; even cancelling your credit cards and dealing with your mail...tying up some or all of the loose ends. An executor may be a family member, friend, or anyone you believe to be trustworthy and capable of carrying out these important and sometimes complicated tasks. **Some states have specific requirements for executors so you may wish to seek professional legal guidance when deciding on an executor—and of course talk to your executor as soon as you make your choice to make sure they're ok with taking on these critical duties (and tell them where they'll be able to find all of your assets when the time comes!).**

A **Trust** is likewise a set of instructions for the distribution of assets after death, but may cover more complicated circumstances...so if a will is like a dump truck, a trust may be more like a courier service delivering packages to beneficiaries over time with specific conditions.

For example a trust may stretch distributions to a minor child (or their guardian) throughout their life in the form of regular income, or lump sums at particular ages; a "special needs trust" may provide financial support for a disabled beneficiary in an efficient manner (and may also be designed to reduce disruption of Medicaid assistance); a "charitable remainder trust" may provide support to a surviving spouse, then after that spouse's death distribute what's left to charitable organizations specified in the trust.

There are many other common uses of trusts…essentially any legally permissible instructions you can clearly explain to an attorney can potentially be written into a trust document. Always seek professional legal advice.

A trust may be

- o **Revocable:** you retain control of the assets until death, or

- o **Irrevocable:** you give up control of the assets—they are owned by the trust, the trustee generally controls the assets, and your ability to make changes is very limited.

    For example you *may* be able to change beneficiaries, or change the trustee, or add assets to the trust, or take other limited actions depending on the laws in your state; but you would likely not be able to direct how assets are invested, or take assets directly out of the trust yourself.

    Again, always seek professional legal guidance as rules may vary by state.

So why would you want to give up control of your assets to an irrevocable trust? There are many possible uses for this arrangement; for example, to shelter assets from Medicaid spend-down rules for long-term care situations. However this likely will *not* avoid potential Medicaid "look-back" rules—seek legal guidance!—but if you put assets into an irrevocable trust and then survive through the State-required look-back period (typically five years as of this writing, but check with your attorney), Medicaid may not consider assets in the trust as available for your expenses, thus potentially protecting that amount of your assets for your trust beneficiaries.

Again, get professional legal guidance, and update your will and trust as needed, as Congress may change laws at any time.

Another example: if your estate value exceeds the U.S. estate tax exclusion, you may look into an irrevocable trust as a way to potentially shelter assets from estate tax for your heirs; again, seek professional legal guidance as laws may change frequently in this area.

Another example: a "special-needs trust" may provide income to a disabled person within certain thresholds designed not to disrupt Medicaid qualification. Seek legal assistance.

For both revocable and irrevocable trusts, you must designate a trustee or trustees to carry out a trust's provisions. Like the executor of a will, this person is responsible for a number of important activities—but unlike a will which generally must be fulfilled within a relatively short timeframe depending on the State, a trust may require long-term management. For this reason, you may want to consider using a trust company, trust attorney, or other professional as your trustee. Funding for trustee services may be included in the trust itself. Seek professional legal guidance.

A properly written trust *does* avoid probate for your assets…but again, a trust is not necessary if that's your only goal (see "*Nothing Should Go Through Probate!*" section for alternatives).

One more time: always seek professional guidance.

The Power Of Stepped-Up Basis

If you sell an appreciated asset during your lifetime, you pay capital gains tax. For example, if a piece of real estate was worth $100,000 when you bought it (your "basis" in the property), and you later sell it for $150,000, you may owe capital gains tax on the $50,000 increase in value. (Get professional guidance from your accountant for your own situation.)

But if instead you pass the property to an heir, the heir's "stepped-up basis" will be the $150,000 value at the time of your death (or under the "alternate valuation" rule as of this writing, the value six months after death…but *only if* this valuation would result in a lower *estate tax* bill).

In this scenario your heir would pay *no* capital gains if they immediately sold the property for $150,000. If instead they sold it later for $170,000, they would only be liable for capital gains tax on the $20,000 gain above their stepped-up basis.

Needless to say this provision of the IRS code has significant ramifications for estate planning. If you want to give your heirs an appreciated asset you purchased years ago (or one you think will appreciate in the future), and there's no urgency to the gift, they may come out much better from a "net gift" standpoint if you leave it to them after you die instead of during your life.

Seek guidance from a qualified tax professional.

IRA Beneficiaries (Including Tax Considerations)

IMPORTANT: Get professional guidance—IRS rules may change at any time, so don't depend on yesterday's information in this book or anywhere else.

There are several options (and potential pitfalls) when you select your IRA beneficiaries, with potentially enormous tax and income planning consequences for heirs.

- There may be a significant difference in tax treatment, and required distribution rules, if a spouse is named as primary beneficiary, versus a non-spouse.

- Whether or not the deceased taxpayer had already starting taking IRS Required Minimum Distributions (RMD's) may also affect requirements for the inheriting spouse. The age of the inheriting spouse compared to the age of the deceased spouse can also make a difference in the distribution rules; as can the registration of the account as a "Beneficiary IRA" versus "Traditional IRA." Again, work closely with your advisor and/or tax professional to make sure you're getting up-to-date information.

- As with any asset, avoid probate and other unintended consequences for your heirs by making sure you have correctly named primary *and* contingent beneficiaries...and keep them updated. If you inherit an IRA, make sure you do the same thing for your new account.

- Get a copy of the beneficiary form for each account (IRA's and otherwise), keep them in a safe place, and *tell your beneficiaries where those are located.* This may also be a good opportunity to share a little of your knowledge about this topic with your heirs, and set them on the road to a solid financial plan of their own.

- If you live in a community property state, special considerations apply. For example your spouse *must* be your primary beneficiary in most circumstances unless they explicitly give up that right (notarized signature may be required). Get advice from an experienced professional who understands the rules in your State.

- Never name your estate as beneficiary. The IRA may go through probate and may have to be distributed over a shorter timeframe—and perhaps with significant tax consequences. Seek professional guidance.

- Naming a trust as IRA beneficiary is tricky, as the receiving trust must contain certain very specific provisions in order to preserve tax deferral. Work with an attorney who is experienced in writing this type of trust in your State. Also keep in mind that trusts may be subject to higher tax rates than individuals…again, seek professional and experienced tax and/or legal counsel to explore your options for trusts inheriting IRA's…it's a minefield!

- In the past, an heir could put the money from an inherited IRA in the bank, spend some of it, replace the spent money, then proceed to rolling it into their own IRA and avoid tax consequences—*but this has changed*…as of this writing, the transfer must be directly between the company who is custodian of the IRA and the receiving company (a "trustee-to-trustee transfer"). Once again, make sure you're getting professional advice based on current tax law, which changes frequently.

Other IRA beneficiary concepts:

If an IRA passes to a young beneficiary, the ultimate result may be a *very* long total period of tax deferral, starting with the original tax deductible IRA contributions, continuing through the life of the surviving spouse, and potentially through the life of the *next* beneficiary…but check current tax law, as Congress can change laws at any time.

This could mean a potentially *astounding* number of years of compounding tax deferral.

If a surviving spouse is "pre-retirement" age under IRS rules (under age 59 ½ as of this writing) and needs to use the IRA money, there may be provisions allowing the surviving spouse to treat the IRA as an "inherited IRA," instead of treating it as a traditional IRA…and therefore potentially avoiding IRS penalties for pre-retirement distributions. **But be very careful of how the account is registered so it is clearly designated as an "inherited IRA"—get professional guidance.**

Extra care should be taken when beneficiaries take distributions from any IRA, as this may be treated as ordinary income by the IRS, potentially increasing their tax liability.

Roth IRA's (funded with after-tax money) may receive entirely different treatment, so proceed carefully and seek professional advice as always. For example, the timeframe when a Roth IRA is first started may have a much different impact on the tax picture when compared to a traditional IRA.

A spouse who receives a traditional IRA from their deceased spouse may want to consider converting it to a Roth IRA after the transfer, if this provides advantages under current tax law. This only works if other non-IRA funds are available to pay income tax on the converted amount—for example life insurance payouts which are not needed for other purposes. An advantage of a Roth IRA at the time of this writing is that no further tax will be due on the principal, nor on any subsequent growth, and there are no required distributions for an inheriting spouse (but there *are* required distributions for non-spouse heirs), so spousal heirs can leave the money to grow Federal and State tax-free. This may be especially beneficial for a surviving spouse who expects to be in a higher tax bracket later on, and therefore wants to entirely avoid future taxes on the account.

Non-spouse beneficiaries of IRA's face enough options and tax consequences to fill a separate book. Seek professional advice.

A non-spouse beneficiary may disclaim the IRA entirely...just say "no thanks" (partially or entirely). This may be appropriate if for example the beneficiary is financially better off than when the deceased IRA owner originally selected beneficiaries, and the next beneficiary in line, perhaps another family member, needs the money more (and may also be in a lower tax bracket—which may make disclaiming the IRA a better choice than simply accepting the money, paying income tax, and gifting the remaining amount).

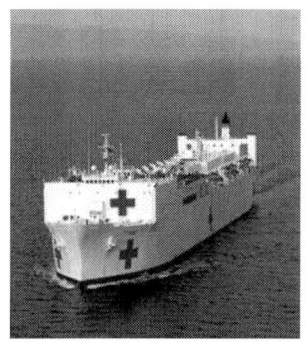

Naming a non-profit or church as the beneficiary of your IRA is another option to consider. Under current tax law at the time of this publication, the money may be distributed tax free (Federal and State tax-free), providing maximum benefit to the charity. If your estate is large enough to be subject to estate tax, leaving your IRA to a charity may remove that amount from your taxable estate. This could potentially reduce the tax burden for your other heirs. **Work with your accountant to comply with current tax law and to determine the effect on your own situation.**

We and many of our clients contribute considerable time and resources, including money, to great charitable causes, churches and related mission work, colleges, and other worthy causes. As we've mentioned elsewhere in this book, you might be amazed to learn how slim the operating margin is for many excellent local nonprofits. A gift of life insurance proceeds or other assets can mean even more to them than you might expect.

Such gifts can be part of a sensible financial planning strategy, and part of leaving a proud legacy. Giving of yourself and your wealth is a way to make a very real and potentially critical and lasting difference for others…and ultimately perhaps leave the world a little bit better than you found it.

Estate Planning For Business Owners

Review "Risk Management For Business Owners" near the end of the Risk Management chapter for a discussion of business contingency planning concepts, including death of the owner. There we talk about identifying and preparing your successor; buy-sell agreements to facilitate the transition to new ownership, which may include provisions for purchase of the business from a surviving spouse; funding of the buy-sell agreement through life insurance or other means; stay-put agreements with key employees including monetary "teeth" to motivate them to stick with the company through a transition; and the critical task of preparing your successor *now* to be able to take over effectively when the time comes—whether that's triggered by death or retirement.

Work with tax and legal professionals to consider estate planning pros and cons of your business entity type (sole proprietorship, partnership, LLC, S-corp, etc.) to be sure it fits your goals.

Beyond those special considerations, the estate planning concepts discussed throughout this chapter may apply to your business as with any other asset. Review your estate plan with your attorney and business accountant to ensure that you've properly addressed company-specific aspects of your estate tax and gift tax exposure; probate avoidance provisions; your will, trust, powers of attorney, and other estate planning documents—and discuss with your planning professionals the potential capital gains tax benefits of stepped-up basis for heirs, versus transfer of company ownership during your lifetime via gifts, installment sale, or other means.

A Final Estate Planning Cautionary Tale

This estate planning story is from John's own family, so we'll let him tell it:

"My wife Diana and I grew up in St. Louis. Diana's dad was a talented and successful carpenter who died too young in his late 50's. Diana's mom Edith remarried in 1980 and spent nineteen very happy years with Clois before she died.

She and Clois had each brought about $500,000 into the marriage, and four children each.

Clois and Edith had agreed from the beginning that when they passed, everything should go the kids in equal shares. When Edith died, the burden of carrying out this commitment fell to Clois.

Clois had been a well-regarded executive in the private sector before retirement, so we were confident he was capable of making the proper arrangements. By this time I was an experienced financial advisor, so I respectfully referred Clois to a couple of competent attorneys in St. Louis who could help him write (or update) his trust if needed. He was a kind man, but also very private, especially when it came to his finances...but he nodded and thanked me, and assured me everything was taken care of.

When Clois died in 2003 there were eight bank CD's of approximately equal value, one in each of the kids' names. The balance of the estate consisted of a few smaller cash accounts in banks, and a house in St. Louis.

To our surprise, Clois' attorney informed us there was no trust, and no provisions in Clois' will to sell his assets at his death. In order for the house to be sold so that the value could be distributed, all eight brothers and sisters would need to sign an agreement. Unfortunately the executor of the will—one of those eight siblings—lived out of town, traveled extensively, and was going through a divorce, so this process did not take priority for him.

Eventually the signatures were obtained, but other delays followed, the house sat on the market for two years—and wasn't properly maintained through all of this, so it fell into a state of disrepair. Ultimately the house, the centerpiece of Clois and Edith's legacy, sold for about half of what its value had been at Clois' death.

So this relatively simple estate ended up taking about three-and-a-half years to settle, and cost the heirs close to $150,000 in lost value, attorney fees, and other costs. All of it completely avoidable.

The sad reality was that Clois—a good man, and a frugal man—had decided to save the modest cost of basic estate planning documents, and instead wrote his own will.

I tell this story to illustrate the irony and "false economy" we see far too often, where well-meaning folks skip the expense of professional financial advice to save a few bucks. And I tell this story because this was our own family, and I saw up-close how disheartening and stressful this period was for Diana and her seven brothers and sisters.

So tell your advisors what is really going on in your life. Share what you think you can do yourself, and what you want the results to be. Be open to hearing how we might be able to assist.

That's why we're here. Let us help you."

7.

Retirement Planning

Younger clients are concerned about making and accumulating money. Clients heading into retirement are trying to figure out how to sustain the next thirty years without running out of it.

-John Piatchek

BOTTOM LINE: Seek balance between current lifestyle needs, wants, and dreams, and the planning and savings requirements necessary to fulfill future retirement needs, wants, and dreams.

If you're not yet retired, come up with reasonable projections of what retirement might look like for you, and what it will require in terms of income and resources. Work backward from that to estimate how much you need to be saving to attain your goals. Recalculate on a regular basis to make sure you're on track and to account for changes to your retirement expectations.

Online tools may be sufficient in early life stages, but seek professional assistance if you are closer to retirement, or already in retirement. Account for inflation, and evaluate "bad-case" scenarios that may help you plan for the unexpected (early death of a spouse, large emergency expenditure, higher-than-projected inflation or lower-than-expected growth on investments, etc.).

Take full advantage of tax deferral and company contributions if you are able to participate in a workplace retirement plan (and accept planning assistance from your workplace plan's investment company if it's offered).

Business owners: seek early professional guidance for exit planning tactics to help increase the value of your business now, and put plans in place to facilitate a lucrative and smooth transition to family, employees, or third parties.

Understand investment products and risk tolerance concepts (see Investing chapter): the long-term rate of growth of your retirement savings can potentially affect your progress, and ultimately the quality of your retirement.

When you're within a few years of needing to draw from retirement accounts, implement our Recession Reserve™ asset allocation approach (see Investing chapter).

As retirement approaches, and throughout retirement, create a detailed retirement budget. Again, include both basic needs and lifestyle wants and dreams.

Seek professional assistance to help maximize your Social Security benefits; understand Social Security delaying and spousal claiming strategies, and how those strategies could affect the surviving spouse in case of a death. Know the negative ramifications of receiving employment income and claiming Social Security simultaneously before full retirement age.

Plan for tax-efficient use of retirement assets. Don't jump the gun *on raiding tax-advantaged accounts.*

Avoid enormous penalties by taking IRS Required Minimum Distributions from tax-deferred accounts (IRA's etc.) starting at age 70 ½ (work with your tax professional for current rules).

Adjust risk management strategies and products as needed; make sure your estate planning documents are updated, and revisit your legacy planning.

Revisit your retirement projections periodically (both before and during retirement) to see if reality matches the projections—then adjust both the reality and the projections as needed.

Take advantage when the U.S. dollar is relatively stronger than other currencies to leverage lower-cost world travel.

Your final "bottom line" required task:
   It's your future…you earned it. So enjoy!

THE TEAM

Almost everyone needs sooner or later:
   Financial planning professional
   Investment professional (some CFP®, ChFC or other financial
      planning professionals are qualified for this role).

   Accountant
   Attorney
   Life insurance professional
   Property and casualty insurance professional
   Health insurance professional

And in some life stages:
   Medicare supplement agent

Long-term care insurance professional

And for some:
Real estate broker/agent
Business exit and succession planning specialist

DO-SOME-OF-IT-YOURSELFERS: Like most aspects of financial planning, building a retirement plan is a cooperative effort between you and your team. There are lots of online saving and budgeting tools available for retirement planning, in addition to the resources your professional advisors can provide.

Figure out what you want retirement to look like…it's not just an extended two-week vacation that never ends. You must find satisfying activities to occupy your free time, and organize your obligations to family and others to get everything done (many say they have less "free time" in retirement than they did before!). Once you're clear on how you want retirement to play out, work with your advisors to plan for the funding, tax management, risk management, legacy planning, and estate planning aspects of your strategy.

How it works in the real world: Mr. and Mrs. T (no, not that Mr. T) came to us feeling their financial lives were disorganized ahead of retirement—that they were not as "in tune" and informed as they wanted to be. Their investments were "fractured" in pieces with various companies; they weren't sure when to claim Social Security; and they were worried about the state of the economy, with little confidence that the world would get better anytime soon.

We showed this lovely couple our Survivors Guide, a sort of family financial scrapbook to help them get organized (see a description of the Survivors Guide near the end of the Building A Plan chapter).

We analyzed their Social Security benefits and provided instructions for a claiming strategy to help maximize their retirement income.

We discussed our Recession Reserve™ approach to asset allocation, and made sure they had plenty of liquidity to get through a typical recession (or even a worse-than-average one), without having to sell stock funds at a loss during a market downturn. This allocation aligned with their sense of their own risk tolerance, so they could sleep at night.

We called them periodically throughout that first year with updates of course, and they seemed appreciative of their new-found direction.

On one of those calls we made during a period of some market volatility, Mrs. T told us they were enjoying a trip out of town, that she had started to check the stock markets, but stopped herself and said, "No, my advisor's got this."

"I Wish We Hadn't Saved So Much For Retirement..."

...Said no one, ever. Having more than enough resources to meet all of your retirement goals is not something you would regret.

On the other hand, it is possible to scrimp and sacrifice to such a degree that you may give up more comfort today than may be necessary for your future comfort. We knew a couple who kept the thermostat so low in the winter that they sat bundled up and shivering on the couch, with no television because they thought they should save instead of replacing the one that quit…and all this despite the fact that by this time they actually did have plenty of retirement savings to meet their goals. They just didn't know for sure whether they were on track, so for far too long they erred on the side of misery.

As with much of life, it's about finding balance. Careful, detailed, and ongoing financial planning, including retirement planning, can help you save enough…and also enjoy life along the way.

If You Are Not Yet Close To Retirement…

If you're nowhere near retirement, it may be difficult to imagine what your retirement will look like, or cost.

If you are on a specific career path which you expect to continue, start by finding out how much people earn who are in a late stage of the same career—a stage you can imagine achieving yourself by then.

Use that projected pre-retirement income, and the kind of lifestyle you imagine for yourself with that level of income, as a starting point for estimating your retirement income need. A common rule of thumb is that you may need in retirement about 80% of what you earned right before retirement. The thinking is that once you retire you may no longer have some work-related expenses like work clothes, transportation, lunches out, contributions to a workplace retirement savings plan, and other expense items.

However—and this is critical—your actual spending needs will depend largely on what you intend to do for fun in the first 15-20 years of retirement, and other factors specific to your own situation. So the "80% rule" may or may not be a good rule of thumb for you.

Will you travel the world? Or just do some local fishing and hiking? Or deep sea fishing requiring a lot of pricey gear and a big boat (and will you buy or rent?)?

Perhaps you intend to start a rock band after retirement, and incidentally earn a little money on weekends? How long will that likely continue, and what new or additional expenses will that bring? If you have to have a '58 Les Paul collector's guitar to properly rock out, will you even manage to break even?

Again, it's difficult when retirement is a long time away to know just what your interests will be by then. You can only make your best guess about activities you do now that you expect to continue or expand in later years, and perhaps plug in some extra cushion for expenses you can't predict right now. Then adjust the projection periodically as your long-term goals become clearer.

Retirement Accumulation Planning

Once you're as clear as you can reasonably be in regard to your retirement activities, it's time to figure out how much you need to be saving for retirement right now.

If you're able, engage the services of a qualified financial planning professional to do this complicated number crunch.

The next best thing: some workplace retirement plans include access to online retirement planning calculators provided by the investment company. An internet search will find many other such calculators…and some are better than others. Many of them merely show how much you need to save per paycheck (or per month or per year), at an assumed rate of investment growth, to end up with an account balance of a particular size.

Some go an extra step to show how much income you may be able to generate in retirement from that projected lump sum.

Others are more robust, allowing you to enter an inflation rate (a critical necessity in our view), more than one income source (spouse, part time employment in retirement, etc.), one-time lump sums added in retirement (from sale of real estate for example), and a few even allow adjusting your income need at various stages in retirement…for example at the point you expect to pay off a home mortgage, or expect to do less international travel.

See "Big 10 Retirement Planning Components" for a more complete listing of what you need to consider for long-term retirement accumulation planning…items which ideally you would want to plug into a retirement savings calculator if possible.

Once you know how much you need to be saving, it's like all other types of accumulation planning—you must balance your current basic living expenses and lifestyle "wants" and "wishes" against your long-term goals for big-ticket items…and retirement savings is the biggest of the big-ticket items for many of us. See "Income, Budget, And Accumulation Planning" chapter for ideas and techniques.

If you have access to a tax-deferred savings plan such as a workplace 401(k), 403(b), or Simple IRA, use it. Tax deferral means potentially far more money going into saving for retirement over time than you might otherwise be able to save; and that additional money you would have paid out in taxes is enjoying compound growth potential throughout your savings period. In addition, many people are in a lower tax bracket in retirement than they were during their working years (especially mid- to late-career periods). So when you finally do pay taxes on withdrawals from tax-advantaged accounts in retirement, it may be at a lower tax rate.

If your employer offers a contribution match, *at the very least* take full advantage of that if at all possible. That's "free money," immediately giving your retirement savings a boost and putting more money to work for long-term compounding potential.

There are limits on how much you can contribute to workplace retirement savings plans, although the limits are indexed to increase over time (see HR or a planning professional for current limits). But if you need to save additional money beyond the maximum allowed in your workplace plan, you may be able to add money to a traditional or Roth IRA which you own separately. However there are IRS limits on how much you can earn before being denied the ability to contribute to an IRA, if your workplace offers a retirement savings plan. These limits may change over time so be sure to get current information.

If you are more than five years or so from retirement, think about your investment risk tolerance, and your stock-to-bond allocation in the account, in terms of that timeline. Over longer periods the stock markets offer significant growth potential, even though you'll see more volatility (fluctuations of value), and even occasional downturns in your account value during market corrections and recessions.

If you can ignore those "paper losses"—after all you're not drawing from that account yet, so you won't need to "sell low" when stocks are down—you may wish to include more stock funds, and fewer bond funds which are more stable but may provide much less growth over the long run. Speak with an investment professional about your personal situation before investing.

This is our Recession Reserve™ approach to portfolio allocation (see the Investing chapter for a more thorough description). This may be especially attractive if you are playing catch-up with your retirement savings.

Even if you're on track for your retirement goals, you may be able to save less per paycheck and still meet your retirement goals if you invest aggressively during your accumulation years. But in the end you must invest in a way that lets you sleep at night...if you are very troubled by market downturns, adjust your investment allocation more conservatively, even if that means you must save more per paycheck.

Like much of financial planning, it's about finding balance.

If You're Getting Close To Retirement, Or Already Retired...

We always say it's never too late to plan your finances, but the closer you get to retirement the more difficult it may be to make big adjustments. Get clear now on your fixed and discretionary spending, and your resources for paying those expenses. And revisit your risk management picture to account for events that could derail your plans.

Whether you're close to retirement or already there: review the "Big 10" Retirement Planning Components below, and make any adjustments necessary to get on track and stay on track.

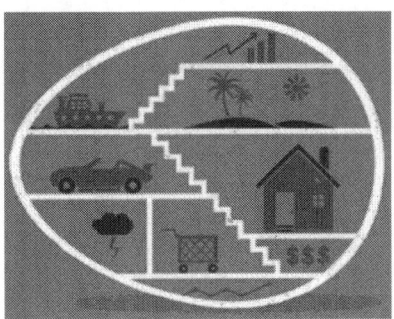

"Big 10" Retirement Planning Components

Below is the big-picture list of items which we believe need to be coordinated within your retirement plan. If your eyes start glazing over at this mere outline when you consider the prospect of trying to do all this yourself, it may be time to meet with a financial advisor.

1. **Retirement itself:** When will you retire? How will you spend your time? How might this change over the course of a 20-30 year retirement? Will you want to relocate at some point—and what will be the difference in the cost of living in that area? What are your goals for sharing your time, and/or your wealth, with others? Do you expect to live a longer or shorter lifespan than average because of family history or health?

2. **Retirement budget:** Separating your retirement needs into a few categories can help you see the big picture, and may make it easier to adjust your strategy if needed...so group retirement budget items using "broad strokes" to see how your long-term plan holds up. There are many ways to approach this...here's a starting point:

    - List **basic living expenses** both large and small, and both regularly occurring and intermittent. Here are the general categories, and your situation may include others...see the Budget List at the end of this book for a more detailed breakdown:
        - Food
        - Clothing
        - Housing and related expenses (mortgage, insurance, taxes, utilities, household/office supplies, maintenance and repair, other?)
        - Health care (insurance, Medicare supplements, copays/deductibles, prescriptions and over the counter medicines, etc.)
        - Personal care (toiletries etc.)
        - Transportation and related expenses (car payments, gas, maintenance and repair, parking, public transportation, etc.)
        - Communication and related expenses (phone service)

- List your **lifestyle "wants"**—items and activities you *could* live without but don't want to:

    Here are some "wants" our own clients have built into their plans:

    - Ocean sailing
    - A sweet three-wheel motorcycle cruiser
    - A new BMW (our client appeared almost to feel guilty about this extravagance—but she deserved it!)
    - Church mission trips to Central America to help develop self-sustaining food resources for orphans
    - World travel to help victims of human trafficking
    - More frequent domestic travel to visit family
    - Supporting a women's college in rural Missouri (which the client attended herself)
    - A trip to Newfoundland
    - Scuba diving

    …and other common "wants":

    - travel
    - dining out and other entertainment expenses
    - hobby expenses and club dues
    - gift-giving
    - college funding for loved ones
    - church or charitable donations, both during life and as part of your legacy planning for when you pass
    - housekeeping service
    - handyman services (if you're not handy enough yourself!)
    - personal cosmetic "upkeep"
    - daughter's wedding (she may say this is a "need"…)

Are things like cable TV, internet, your computer or smartphone "wants" or "needs"? What about higher-priced groceries for gourmet cooking, or a gym membership?

We believe it's helpful to get a grasp of your true baseline needs—what's really the least you could reasonably get by with? If you achieve clarity on this, then you can better plan for worst-case scenarios that life might present.

Could you downgrade to a more basic phone if absolutely necessary? If you consider a car a basic need, could you get by with a lower-priced used car if absolutely necessary? Could you cook less expensively if absolutely necessary? If so, you may want move part of your food budget expense from the "need" list to the "want" list.

These are judgment calls. On the extreme other end of this spectrum—perhaps the *ultimate* "bottom line"—could you survive on little or no money at all? Many in this world do, but we encourage you to draw the line between "need" and "want" at a place that makes reasonable sense for your retirement planning.

- List your **"dreams"**: items and activities you're not sure you can achieve, but would sure like to if possible. Of course dreams are too numerous to list comprehensively...but here are examples (see more in the "Budget List" at the end of the book):

    o   Vacation home, or sun room addition
    o   Relocation
    o   Sports car
    o   Boat
    o   1958 Gibson Les Paul guitar (have we mentioned that elsewhere?)
    o   A work of art (other than the '58 Les Paul)
    o   Flying the family to Everest for an afternoon hike
    o   Leaving a large sum to your favorite non-profit
    o   Cosmetic surgery (is this a want, dream, or "need"?)
    o   Starting a business
    o   Vacation travel currently out of reach

Just because some dreams may seem a bit (or a lot) out of reach, it's worth including them in your plan in case things work out better than expected.

- Apply an **inflation rate** for each type of retirement need. Keep in mind that you may need to apply different inflation rates for basics, health care, college tuition, long-term care, and perhaps other items.

- Finally, account for **expected changes in your needs during retirement**...for example a home mortgage that will be paid off; or perhaps less international travel after age 85 (but only if you're sure you will have had enough by then!).

If you haven't had a series of in-depth conversations with your significant other(s) about all of this, you may wish to do so well ahead of retirement. This may be the most important step of all, and needs to be revisited periodically throughout retirement—the rest is just a great big number crunch!

3. **Income sources:** Consider fixed income sources throughout retirement such as Social Security and pensions; sources which are fixed for a certain period of time—for example rental property income you may foresee giving up in the future; and non-fixed income such as variable investment income or trust income, or part time employment. Be sure to account for COLA's (cost of living adjustments) on Social Security, some pensions, and some financial products (some annuities for example).

    Pension considerations: If you are going to receive a company or government pension, you may be offered a number of options: a lifetime income stream for yourself only, or a smaller amount with a continuing benefit for your surviving spouse. In that case the survivor benefit is usually a percentage of your own benefit—typically 50%, 75%, or 100%, and the more your surviving spouse will receive, the less your own initial benefit will be. These options are based on standard lifespan tables so theoretically the total income should be about the same for each option if you and your spouse both live exactly as long as the average person.

    However we have analyzed many pension offerings, and in some cases one or more of the survivor choices were either extra good or extra poor, so don't base your decision on a coin flip.

Work with your advisor to think through all of the remaining income sources if *either* spouse dies, including the fact that a surviving spouse will receive the equivalent of the higher of the two Social Security benefits, not both amounts. (That fact alone means choosing a pension survivor benefit, and/or implementing a Social Security delayed claiming strategy, may make sense for many couples.)

Then have your advisor analyze your pension options to see which one is optimal. This can be very complicated. One method is to plug each of the various options into separate retirement projections to see how much is left at the end in each case; and then change the lifespan assumptions for each recipient to determine whether income will be sufficient if one spouse dies prematurely.

4. **Assets to be used for retirement needs:** These could include bank accounts, investments, and items of worth such real estate or collectibles you can earmark to cover gaps not funded by other retirement income sources.

   Periodically revisit the costs and performance of your investments…and those two factors are often closely related. The lower the fees in an investment—including hidden trading fees (see the "Investing" chapter to learn about efficient investing)—the better your performance might be, which can be an important factor in planning and meeting your retirement goals.

5. **Risk management:** Some risk management items such as property and casualty insurance overlap with pre-retirement needs—but there are many other considerations in retirement: health care expenses may increase significantly, and health insurance before Medicare eligibility will have to be addressed; Medicare supplement analysis becomes critical as you approach Medicare eligibility age; life

insurance needs may change dramatically; and the need to consider long-term care insurance may be more pressing.

Work with your advisors to understand and address your risks, and include reasonable estimates for out-of-pocket expenses for insurance premiums, copays, deductibles, and other risk management costs in your retirement plan.

6. **Tax and estate planning considerations:** What is the optimal order to distribute funds from tax deferred accounts (IRA's for example), versus taxable accounts?

    How should you manage capital gains from investment sales, in relation to other sources of income, to potentially reduce your tax burden?

    What assets make sense to pass along for heirs to receive "stepped-up basis"? This means a fresh capital gains starting point—for example if you sell stocks which are worth more than what you originally paid for them, the profit may be subject to capital gains tax; but if instead you pass those stocks along to your heirs, at your death the heirs start with a brand new "basis" value and are only subject to capital gains tax on growth from that point forward.

    Are your wills, trusts, powers of attorney, beneficiaries, and other estate planning documents, and your asset titling, all up to date?

    See the Estate Planning chapter for more information.

7. **Legacy planning:** Paying for kids' or grandkids' education, leaving money to your church or favorite non-profit, starting an endowment, etc.—making a lasting difference in the world. If this is important to you, make it part of the plan.

8. **Run the numbers.** Calculate each year's results all the way through your projected lifespan.

We believe it's critical that you also evaluate your results by running "bad-case" scenarios:

- inflation is higher than originally projected
- investment growth is lower than originally projected
- spouse 1 dies prematurely
- spouse 2 dies prematurely
- one or both spouses live much *longer* than expected
- health care expenses are higher than expected
- a disaster scenario occurs, for example a large legal loss or large medical loss not covered by insurance
- Mom or Dad (or other family member?) moves in…or you have to help them with medical, housing, home maintenance, or other expenses
- what else can you think of?

And what if *two* disaster scenarios play out in the same year? Could you still at least meet your basic living expenses? How would you adjust your lifestyle from that point forward to perhaps rescue some of your lifestyle wants and dreams?

Analyzing bad-case scenarios is important for contingency planning, and to expose and address potential areas of risk you may not have considered. It can be emotionally challenging to push these fear buttons, but ironically it may also help you be a little better emotionally prepared for life's curveballs…much like first responders tend to remain calm and find solutions more effectively if they have previously practiced "fire drills." Run your financial fire drills now…and run them again periodically.

How much is left over at the end of your plan projection under "normal" and "fire drill" scenarios? If it's too much (!), maybe you'll want to revisit your legacy planning, or your lifestyle goals, or move those "dreams" into the "wants" column. Or maybe you can afford less volatility/risk (and therefore less potential return) in your investments.

9. **Adjust the plan:** Are there years when your projected resources *don't* meet your needs? This is where you have to get creative…but there are really only six levers you can pull:

- Save more ahead of retirement.

- Spend less during retirement.

- Adjust the timing and/or frequency of expenditures during retirement: for example replace your car every eight years instead of every five years; and perhaps delay the car replacement if you project a new roof on your home will be needed the same year.

- Earn more during retirement—perhaps turn a hobby into an income source?

- Adjust the timing of income-generating activities: sell the real estate or turn on the annuity income rider a year or two sooner for example, or keep the rental property going a little longer than you originally planned.

- Seek more growth potential on your retirement savings. But take care not to push your risk tolerance too far—if you lose sleep because you're more exposed to stock market volatility than you're comfortable with, other adjustments may make more sense for you. Our Recession Reserve™ approach, explained in the Investing chapter, may help you manage your "emotional" risk tolerance against the historical realities of the capital markets if you do need to seek more investment growth potential.

10. **Review and repeat:** Look at your plan periodically and adjust as circumstances and/or projections change. Do this as far in advance as possible before retirement, and again periodically both before and during retirement. Are the projections you came up with before retirement holding up? If you're getting ahead, or behind, make adjustments and re-run the numbers.

Don't Jump The Gun On Drawing From Tax Deferred Accounts!

One of the biggest tax mistakes you can make is to start taking withdrawals from a 401(k), IRA, or other tax deferred account before age 59 ½.

Not only will you end the tax deferral on the money you take out (and the potential growth on both the money and the deferred taxes), and subject yourself to Federal and State income tax on the withdrawal for that year, but you may also be subject to an additional 10% penalty. There are only a few exceptions…for example as of this writing: certain medical or disability expenses; buying, building, or rebuilding a first home; "substantially equal payments" which meet specific requirements; higher education expenses in some limited cases, and a small number of other situations.

Work with your tax accountant to see if your situation may meet current exceptions—and if not, try your best to find other resources.

The Mother Of All Tax Penalties: Missing Your RMD's

The IRS gives us the gift of tax deferral in our qualified retirement plans at work, and in IRA's. Take advantage of that as long as you can. But the IRS won't wait forever—at age 70 ½ in most cases you *must* start taking "required minimum distributions" (RMD's) and pay the piper (the piper is the IRS).

If you don't, the penalty as of this writing is *50% of the amount you should have taken out.* So if your RMD is $1,000, you have to go ahead and take the $1,000 and pay tax…plus an additional $500 penalty. This is one of the all-time biggest tax penalties for U.S. filers.

Depending on where your birthday lands on the calendar, RMD's start at around 3.6% – 3.9% of your account balance as of the end of the previous year (check current rules).

Each subsequent year's RMD is also based on the account balance at the end of the previous year, but the percentage you have to take out (upon which you pay Federal and State income tax) goes up a little every year.

If you have more than one IRA, 401(k), 403(b), or other tax deferred qualified account, the IRS doesn't care whether you take an RMD from each account, or add up all the RMD's and take that total from just one account, or a couple of accounts…they only care whether the total distribution is correct so they get the right amount of tax revenue. Keep good records in case you're ever audited.

It's important to note that if you're still employed at age 70 ½, you're generally *not* subject to required minimum distribution rules for holdings in your employer's retirement savings plan. Talk with a tax or investment professional about your personal situation and current rules.

As of this writing, for your first RMD (the year you turn 70 ½), the IRS allows you to delay until April 1 of the following year. This may come in handy if you expect the RMD to drive you into a higher tax bracket the year you turn 70 ½, and you think you'll do better by shifting that income to the following year; or if you just want to keep tax deferral going as long as possible, or for other reasons.

However even if you delay your first RMD until the year after you turn 70 ½, you are still responsible for taking your second RMD *during* that same year, by December 31…in other words you will be responsible for taking two RMD's that year. This could potentially ruin the advantage of delaying your first RMD at all, so work closely with your tax professional when making this decision.

There are no RMD's for a Roth IRA for the original owner, or for a spouse who inherits the account. However a non-spouse beneficiary does have to take RMD's—which are tax-free, but again with significant penalties for failure to do so each year. Ask your tax preparer about current rules in case they've changed.

Social Security Maximization: The $779,000 Question

Getting more Social Security—or potentially much less depending on how and when you claim—may have a significant effect on your retirement comfort, for the rest of your life.

To replicate a $2,000 monthly Social Security benefit for twenty-five years with a 2.5% annual cost of living adjustment would require a hypothetical $590,000 investment growing at 4% per year.

Certainly if you owned such a large investment you would want to make sure it was well-managed. Your Social Security benefit should get the same attention.

The formula for your Social Security benefit is based on your highest 35 years of earnings, which are then adjusted for wage inflation since each of those years. A formula is then applied to arrive at your "full retirement age" benefit (your "full retirement age" varies depending on year of birth).

You may start taking benefits as early as age 62 if you're willing to potentially give up 25% of your full retirement age monthly benefit—as if your hypothetical $590,000 investment was suddenly less than $443,000.

Or you may wait until as late as age 70 to potentially get up to 32% *more* than your full retirement age Social Security benefit…requiring a hypothetical investment of $779,000 growing at 4% per year to produce an equivalent amount of income.

When you look at it this way, you can see why your Social Security claiming strategy is critical.

Spousal Social Security Claiming Strategies

Under certain circumstances as of this writing (verify current rules with a professional), a spouse with a lower earnings record who reaches full retirement age before starting Social Security may choose to take 50% of the higher earning spouse's benefit instead of taking benefits on their own account, as long as their own benefit isn't higher.

If the lower-earning spouse then delays taking benefits on their own account until age 70, this may dramatically increase their own benefit, thereby ultimately increasing the overall income for the household.

Note: The rules around spousal claiming strategies are complicated, and staff at Social Security Administration offices may or may not be aware of all the rules, so again, it's critical that you work with an experienced professional.

Social Security "Break-Even" Analysis

Delaying Social Security means potentially receiving a higher benefit, but it will take some time before the higher benefit payouts bring in a total amount of money equivalent to what you would have received had you not delayed Social Security...your "break-even" date.

A break-even analysis which also estimates annual Social Security cost of living adjustments is especially important for a retiree who has reason to believe their lifespan may be shorter than average.

The Fatal Journey To The Mailbox

What if you delay Social Security to age 70 to get the maximum benefit, and then die on the way to the mailbox to get your first Social Security check?

Your surviving spouse will receive the equivalent of the higher of their own benefit or yours...so even if the delay did you no good, your surviving spouse may benefit significantly, thanks to your planning.

(And make sure you have a Power Of Attorney in place now so your surviving spouse can actually cash that check you left in the mailbox...without having to get a court order!)

Working v. Social Security Offset

If you earn too much money from working before your full retirement age—while receiving Social Security checks—your Social Security benefit may be dramatically reduced.

As of this writing, the offset is fifty cents for every dollar earned, until the year you reach full retirement age...at which time the reduction is less (to allow for people reaching full retirement age during the year they retire from the workforce).

There are a number of moving parts to this equation, so work with a professional or talk with staff at the Social Security Administration to understand how claiming Social Security while still working can affect your benefits.

After you reach full retirement age (by the Social Security Administration's definition based on your year of birth), you can earn as much money as you wish without affecting your Social Security benefit.

Leverage A Strong Dollar For Cheap Vacations In Retirement!

Check the status of the U.S. dollar any time you make international travel plans. If the U.S. dollar is strong compared to the currency of the country to which you're traveling (in other words one of your dollars buys more of their dollars), that can make international purchases and travel to those weaker-currency locations significantly less expensive.

If the dollar is weak (it takes more of your dollars to buy theirs), the opposite is true. The price of a hotel room, meal, cab, and souvenirs will be higher in terms of the U.S. dollars you take with you.

Retirement And Succession Planning For Business Owners

Thorough discussions of business contingency planning, succession planning, and exit planning are beyond the scope of this book, but they should be an integral part of retirement planning for any entrepreneur, regardless of the size of your business. We touch on these topics throughout the book (pay particular attention to "Special

Investing Considerations For Business Owners" in the Investing chapter); beyond those overviews, seek help from qualified and experienced business planning, tax planning, and business law professionals.

There are many strategies available for a business owner to retire comfortably and pass their company along to family, employees, or third parties…and each approach has its own set of pros and cons, tax ramifications, and potential outcomes.

Get ahead of these issues as early as possible—in fact the day you open your doors for business is not a minute too soon to start thinking about your contingency planning and exit strategy! So get professional guidance as soon as possible.

Create a formal written plan which includes strategies for increasing the value of your business at least five to ten years ahead of your exit date. These strategies can actually provide a template for running a better business at *any* time, so again, start looking at these techniques as early as possible in the life of your business.

It's also important to create a culture of success with your employees, and especially with your key employees…an "ownership mentality" where they see their critical role in the long-term success of the business, and their role in helping the business continue with or without you.

Again, seek advice from experienced business planning professionals.

We Have Bad News…And Good News…

…Sometimes with the same client on the same day, sometimes with two different clients, and that's just part of financial planning. Your goals come first, then we see if you're on track to meet those goals, and the chips fall where they may.

When we perform a retirement analysis, we may have a sense of how it's going to turn out because we've done so many. But even we're surprised sometimes. For example this may happen when a client decides not to tell us up front about all of their assets, and when the retirement projections come up short they may say, "Well add this in!" and it may make all the difference.

Sometimes it's the client who is more surprised than we are.

When we met with Mrs. V, a referral from another long-time client, she thought she had it all worked out. She had a 401(k) from her years of employment at a local (world-famous) sporting goods store, and in addition she had inherited a lump sum from her deceased husband's State deferred compensation program.

Her plan was to plow through both accounts and then move in with her adult daughter's family. They already had a downstairs "mother-in-law" quarters ready to go.

But the reasons Mrs. V originally came to see us had nothing to do with that—she was interested in learning about life insurance, long term care, and bypassing probate for her heirs. In the course of our conversation she mentioned her retirement strategy in passing, half-joking about the gift of a tricycle she gave her little girl when she was a toddler, and how someday Mrs. V herself would be the "third wheel" in her daughter's home.

Her language revealed a discomfort with this plan. We asked if she knew how long it would be before the two retirement accounts would run dry. She said thought she had some idea, but wasn't sure, and asked if we could calculate that for her.

When we met again, we showed Mrs. V a projected outcome using recent performance numbers on the two accounts. The money would be depleted in about twenty years, around Mrs. V's age of seventy-nine. A shadow seemed to pass across her eyes as she contemplated this. She expected to have a long lifespan, and the prospect of having to move in with the kids didn't seem like such a joking matter this time.

We showed her an alternative, a way to leverage the two accounts using a combination of strategic withdrawals and a product which included an income rider, in a way that would meet her income needs. Guaranteed for life. Any guarantee is only as good as the issuing company, and this was a highly rated company with a strong track record, which we had used in the past with good results.

This meant that Mrs. V could still move in with her daughter if she wanted, any time. Because they had that nice space downstairs ready to go, and she was welcome and loved. But she would never *have to* move there. She could maintain her independence, if she wanted to. She could stay in the home she build with her husband over many decades of hard work, if she wanted to.

That day, for that client, we had good very news. That day was a very good day for her.

And it was a very good day for us too. Not just because of the prospect of engaging with a new client, but because we're only human, and delivering good news makes our day. We had a small part in painting a picture of a different potential future for Mrs. V than she had previously imagined. A better future.

She earned it, and now she could have it.

A Final Word

This book does not cover every topic of study for financial planning…obtaining a CFP® or ChFC or other professional designation requires working knowledge of a much broader range of concepts beyond the scope of this book.

Our goal was not to cover every possible subject in-depth, but to address common and critical financial planning items for individuals and families, and to some degree business owners; to help provide a basis upon which you and your advisors can build a solid plan.

We have encouraged you throughout to seek additional professional guidance. Whether you engage with us, or with advisors to whom you were referred by someone you trust, we strongly encourage you to build your own team of competent financial advisors to build upon the groundwork we establish for you in this book.

We wish you great success in your financial endeavors, and in every other aspect of your life.

And never forget: it's your future…you earned it. It begins now!

IMPORTANT: The opinions expressed in this book are those of the author and may not necessarily reflect those held by Kestra Investment Services, LLC or Kestra Advisory Services, LLC.

This is for general information only and is not intended to provide specific investment advice or recommendations for any individual. Consult your financial professional, attorney, or tax advisor with regard to your individual situation.

Comments concerning past investment performance are not intended to be forward-looking and should not be viewed as an indication of future results.

Please note that all investments are subject to market and other risk factors, which could result in loss of principal.

APPENDIX:

The Budget List

Here is a detailed checklist of items to help with your budget planning, including your retirement budget planning.

Group smaller budget items by how critical they are to your survival and comfort on a scale of 1-10, and separately rank large single items the same way. With this method you can adjust your goals in an organized way as your plan comes into focus. And if that ultimately means making tough decisions, it's easier to see where cuts may hurt less (or more).

1. **"Needs":** Importance to you is 8, 9, or 10 on a scale of 1-10; these are things you just can't do without. It may be helpful to subdivide these items so you don't forget anything—here's a checklist of "basics," "health care," "debt payments," and "big ticket basics."

   - **Basic living expenses:** groceries, household and personal care items, insurance, pet care, transportation (including gas, maintenance, repairs, parking, etc.), phone, regular home and car maintenance, and _____ (other).

     Paid "out of pocket"
     - Groceries
     - Clothing
     - Personal care items (toiletries, etc.)
     - Household supplies
     - Everyday transportation costs including gas, parking, registration and licensing, maintenance, and repairs (you'll need to either look up average annual repair costs for your vehicles, or make a fair estimate based on your experience)
     - Insurance (monthly, quarterly, or annual premiums)

- Other?

Paid monthly or quarterly
- Mortgage
- Utilities
- Car payments
- Other debt payments
- Insurance (homeowners, car, health, life, long-term care, professional, home warranty, other?)

Paid annually
- Taxes (income, property, etc.)
- Some insurance policies

Paid as needed:
- Taxes
- Home maintenance, repair, and equipment replacement: how frequently will you need these, and how much will it cost each time, with inflation?
- Roof
- Siding
- Heating / air conditioning system
- Carpet / flooring
- Appliances including water heaters
- Other home-related items

- **Health Care:** Although health care is a basic living expense, put that in its own separate category, if for no other reason than to enter an appropriate rate of inflation—health care costs have historically risen at a dramatically higher rate than other budget items, and you should account for that if your planning tools allow.

    A good advisor will be able to enter Medicare expense averages for residents of your state, but of course your actual experience in retirement will vary depending on developments you can't predict.

    - Medicare supplement premiums

- Copays
- Deductibles
- Other out-of-pocket expenses
- Over-the-counter medications

- **Debt payments:** Debt payments are budget necessities, but your plan should account for payments which decrease or disappear at some point. (This is another reason it may be difficult to build a *thorough* do-it-yourself retirement plan.)

- **Big-Ticket Basics:** Considering single big-ticket necessities separately allows some pricing wiggle room to adjust your long-term picture, and also lets you see how cash flow may be affected. For example can you afford both a roof and a new car during the same year, and still take your two annual trips for fun? Or can you adjust one of those big items forward or back in time a bit for the sake of your cash flow? Here are a few examples:

  - **Big ticket basic 1:** Replace car every ___ years.
  - **Big-ticket basic 2:** Replace roof every ___ years.
  - **Big ticket basic 3:** New furniture every ___ years.
  - **Bick ticket basic 4:** Replace heating/air unit every ___ years.
  - Etc.

2. **"Wants":** Importance of 4-7 on a scale of 1-10. These are discretionary lifestyle expenses that you see as pretty important for an enjoyable retirement, but you may be willing to adjust the amount of resources dedicated to these items. For large single-ticket "wants," it may be that you either get them or you don't—or perhaps you can adjust the size of the expense, for example downgrade your sports car "want" from a Lamborghini to a (mere) Ferrari.

   Here are other examples:

- **"Everyday" lifestyle items:** Cable TV, eating out and other minor entertainment items, minor-to-medium gifts, club dues, hobby expenses, collecting, and _____?
- **Big-ticket lifestyle item 1:** _____
- **Big-ticket lifestyle item 2:** _____
- Etc.

  Big-ticket lifestyle items might include a boat, sports car (or a new sports car every ___ years), vacation home, paying for a daughter's wedding (although she might argue this is an "essential"!), big gifts, big donations to church or charity, major furniture purchases, hosting a family reunion every ___ years.

  As with "needs," try to separate this group of expenses you consider to be "near-necessities" from *actual* necessities in case it turns out your resources aren't sufficient to meet all of your goals. When push comes to shove you might decide you can eat out a little less often if it means being able to meet other goals.

3. **"Dreams":** Importance 1-3 on a scale of 1-10. The difference between a "want" and a "dream" is just a matter of degree…perhaps you're simply more willing to sacrifice a "dream" than a "want." Here are examples.

    o Vacation home, or sun room addition
    o Relocation
    o Sports car
    o Boat
    o 1958 Gibson Les Paul guitar (have we mentioned that elsewhere?)
    o A work of art (other than the '58 Les Paul)
    o Flying the family to Everest for an afternoon hike
    o Leaving a large sum to your favorite non-profit
    o Cosmetic surgery
    o Starting a business
    o Vacation travel currently out of reach

On the other hand, you don't necessarily want to eliminate a dream item from your plan entirely, even if it doesn't look feasible to meet that goal as of now. If for example your investments do better than expected, or you receive a windfall from an inheritance, or other goals and projections change, you may get that dream vacation home back on your radar after all.

Again, analyzing these three budget zones separately can provide insight into where adjustments might make sense in your planning. Work with your advisor, and revisit your budget periodically.

NOTES

ABOUT THE AUTHOR

Springfield, MO native Kenny Gott, CFP®, SPHR, assists clients at Piatchek & Associates with investments, financial and retirement planning, insurance research and analysis, and other strategic advisory services.

Since 1998 Kenny has also administered pensions, 401(k) plans, stock options, and other retirement programs for Fortune 500 companies, advising hundreds of employees and executives on their retirement plans and other benefits, risk management, and effective leadership and performance management practices.

When he's not working for clients or the community, Kenny is a songwriter and guitarist, and enjoys family time with wife Tina (our Bookkeeper) and daughter Amanda.

Made in the USA
San Bernardino, CA
14 March 2017